"If I face a critical, life-threa
cian who is well versed in th
compassionate, and who res
can coach me on the right q

make practical decisions. In short, I will want Dr. Butler. She will guide me to come to the end of life in a way that commends the gospel and brings glory to God. If she is not available, I will want to reread this book."

John Dunlop, MD, Internal Medicine Doctor, Geriatrics, Yale School of Medicine; author, *Finishing Well to the Glory of God*

"Dr. Butler has done a masterful job in giving us a clear and comprehensive guide to navigating the difficult and complex waters of end-of-life care. Although *Between Life and Death* is written with patients and their families in mind, this book is a welcome and valuable resource for guiding Christian healthcare students through these challenging issues, in addition to providing the necessary biblical grounding and foundations."

Bill Reichart, Vice President of Campus and Community Ministries, Christian Medical & Dental Associations

"It is inevitable that at some point, each one of us will face difficult or even heartbreaking medical decisions. We may have to make decisions related to our own care or, even tougher, the care of someone we love. To prepare to make such decisions in a distinctly Christian way, you won't do better than to read *Between Life and Death*. It will inform, encourage, strengthen, and equip you to act in ways that honor our humanity while bringing glory to our God."

Tim Challies, blogger, Challies.com

"Some of our weightiest decisions wait until the end. When death draws close, what medical treatments will we embrace or reject? Even Jesus-loving Christians struggle to know how to answer these questions, and we need a seasoned doctor to educate us on the options and their pros and cons. Dr. Butler educates the mind, answers the questions, and takes the imagination on an unforgettable ride, made vivid with the descriptive prose only a gifted writer and experienced trauma surgeon could offer us. This remarkable, Christ-centered book is loaded with reality checks and soul checks, and it will serve Christians and pastors for many years to come as they make these final decisions out of faith and not fear."

Tony Reinke, journalist; author, *12 Ways Your Phone Is Changing You*

"Dr. Butler has written a remarkable, unique, and timely book. Combining her medical expertise with biblical compassion and moral evaluation, she lucidly explains what we need to know about life-and-death medical situations. She does not offer vague advice, but grounds her counsel in medical facts, legal realities, spiritual principles, and real-life illustrations."

Douglas Groothuis, Professor of Philosophy, Denver Seminary; author, *Walking Through Twilight: A Wife's Illness—A Philosopher's Lament*

"This is a marvelous book. Dr. Butler, a Christian intensive-care specialist, has woven together a clear explanation of detailed and complex medical issues with an intimate knowledge of Scripture to bring forth a book of immense value for patients, loved ones, and clergy as they face the seemingly insurmountable questions of ICU and end-of-life care. It is well written, illustrated with real-life dilemmas, and oozing with compassion, both her own and that of our Savior."

Robert D. Orr, MD, CM, clinical ethicist; author, *Medical Ethics and the Faith Factor*

"As a pastor's wife, a parent, a daughter, a granddaughter, a friend, a neighbor, and a member of the church, the issues in this book regularly loom over my life and the lives of those around me. How do we best love the sick and dying? How do we know when to pursue medical interventions and when to allow our loved ones to, as Dr. Butler puts it, 'relax into the embrace of Jesus'? These are complex questions without easy answers. But *Between Life and Death* provides a helpful framework of biblical wisdom to illuminate otherwise murky scenarios. Dr. Butler explains the dense medical terminology that can baffle already-overwhelmed caregivers. And, with unflinching (but not unsympathetic) clarity, she brings us to the bedsides of the suffering and tells us what it is like to experience CPR, a ventilator, or artificially administered nutrition. The actual impact and likely outcome of such treatments is far from the glamorous glow of TV medical dramas, but we need to know the stark reality in order to make God-honoring and merciful choices for ourselves and our loved ones. Thankfully, this book also has an expiration date. One day, gathered in the near presence of Christ, we will no longer need to know how to make decisions about death. But in the meantime, I'm glad to have this book on my shelf."

Megan Hill, author, *Praying Together* and *Contentment*; Editor, The Gospel Coalition

"For all the blessings of modern critical care, we have not sufficiently reckoned with its dark underside: what happens when medical technology and intervention do not preserve life but prolong death? With her keen medical training and experience on display, Dr. Kathryn Butler parts the curtain on an array of life-threatening situations that might befall us or those we love. In *Between Life and Death*, Dr. Butler points us to the hope of the gospel, showing what Christian discipleship might look like in some of the most agonizing moments in life. May this book serve as a useful guide and conversation starter as we prepare for death and gaze on Christ."

Ivan Mesa, Books Editor, The Gospel Coalition

"Dr. Kathryn Butler *has ta*ken her Christ-centered life as well as her experiences as a trauma surgeon to give the reader ways to assess end-of-life decisions to the glory of God in Christ Jesus. Her book emphasizes that we live by the grace of God in Christ Jesus. Dr. Butler has included numerous Bible references that are extremely helpful within the context of living and dying in Jesus Christ. It is a must-read for all Christians, church leaders, and medical professionals who are living through end-of-life dilemmas."

Bob Weise, Professor Emeritus of Practical Theology, Concordia Seminary

BETWEEN LIFE and DEATH

BETWEEN LIFE and DEATH

A GOSPEL-CENTERED GUIDE TO END-OF-LIFE MEDICAL CARE

KATHRYN BUTLER, MD

WHEATON, ILLINOIS

Between Life and Death: A Gospel-Centered Guide to End-of-Life Medical Care
Copyright © 2019 by Kathryn Butler

Published by Crossway
      1300 Crescent Street
      Wheaton, Illinois 60187

All rights reserved. No part of this publication may be reproduced, stored in a retrieval system, or transmitted in any form by any means, electronic, mechanical, photocopy, recording, or otherwise, without the prior permission of the publisher, except as provided for by USA copyright law. Crossway® is a registered trademark in the United States of America.

Published in association with the literary agency of Wolgemuth & Associates, Inc.

Cover design: Tim Green, Faceout Studios

Cover image: Shutterstock

First printing 2019

Printed in the United States of America

Scripture quotations are from the ESV® Bible (The Holy Bible, English Standard Version®), copyright © 2001 by Crossway, a publishing ministry of Good News Publishers. Used by permission. All rights reserved.

Trade Paperback ISBN: 978-1-4335-6101-6
ePub ISBN: 978-1-4335-6104-7
PDF ISBN: 978-1-4335-6102-3
Mobipocket ISBN: 978-1-4335-6103-0

Library of Congress Cataloging-in-Publication Data
Names: Butler, Kathryn, 1980- author.
Title: Between life and death : a gospel-centered guide to end-of-life medical care / by Kathryn Butler.
Description: Wheaton, Illinois : Crossway, [2019] | Includes bibliographical references and index.
Identifiers: LCCN 2018033721 (print) | LCCN 2018047922 (ebook) | ISBN 9781433561023 (pdf) | ISBN 9781433561030 (mobi) | ISBN 9781433561047
(epub) | ISBN 9781433561016 | ISBN 9781433561047 (ePub) | ISBN 9781433561030 (mobipocket)
Subjects: LCSH: Death—Religious aspects—Christianity. | Medical care—Religious aspects—Christianity.
Classification: LCC BT825 (ebook) | LCC BT825 .B95 2019 (print) | DDC 362.17/5—dc23
LC record available at https://lccn.loc.gov/2018033721

Crossway is a publishing ministry of Good News Publishers.

```
BP      32   31   30   29   28   27   26   25   24   23   22
15   14   13   12   11   10   9    8    7    6    5    4    3
```

To
My patients, whose courage inspired this book.
And to Scott, Jack, and Christie, who
daily remind me of God's love.

CONTENTS

I am sure that neither death nor life, nor angels nor rulers,
nor things present nor things to come, nor powers,
nor height nor depth, nor anything else in all creation,
will be able to separate us from the love of God
in Christ Jesus our Lord.

—Romans 8:38–39

INTRODUCTION

Their nightmare of blood transfusions and emergency surgeries receded into memory with a whisper. As the respiratory therapist removed the tube tethering him to the ventilator, he sputtered, coughed, and squeezed his eyes shut. Then, with an oxygen mask misting his face, his eyes locked with his wife's. For the first time in two weeks, he spoke, his hoarse voice barely audible: "Hi, Hun."

"We've missed you," she answered. Tears welled in her eyes, and her limbs relaxed, like taut petals unfurling. In that moment, the burden of the car accident, and the havoc that had seized them for so many days, seemed to slip like silk from her shoulders.

The nurses and I beamed. Stories like this had drawn us to critical care. After long nights standing vigil over him, turning dials, adjusting medications, and stilling our frantic hearts, his injuries—his shattered liver, his lungs foaming with blood—no longer threatened him. The laboratory results and the ventilator settings no longer dictated his days. God had reunited husband and wife with a draught of air.

While the nurses still reveled in his recovery, I walked into an adjacent room to check on another patient. My joy ebbed as I stepped through the doorway and laid eyes upon the elderly gentleman who withered into his mattress. He relied upon the same battery of machines that had rescued our car accident survivor, yet his illness had assumed a starkly different trajectory. A massive stroke had paralyzed him and obliterated his capacity for language. Jaundice yellowed his skin to the color of turmeric. Bruises mottled his arms as blood leeched into his tissues. Although a formidable array of lines and tubes pumped and churned, his organ function dwindled. He was dying.

As I stood at the doorway, his wife sat beside him with her gaze distant and her hands limp in her lap. We had already spent hours poring over numbers and statistics. We had discussed prognosis, outlook, disease processes, and research. Yet during those long hours, I had failed to address the anguish twisting in her heart.

"Do I have any right to make decisions about his living or dying?" she would ask, as my team and I inquired about whether to continue life support. "Isn't that God's place, not mine? I don't think [my husband] would want any of this, but I don't know what's right." She would search our faces for the reassurance she lacked, and when we offered none, she would place a hand over his to stroke the contours, once so familiar, that disease had bloated beyond recognition.

As I stood in the doorway this time, she did not raise her eyes to greet me. In the dim light, I barely discerned the silvery lines staining her cheeks. She had been crying for a while. "He's the one who usually helps me with hard things like this," she said, with her gaze still fixed on the past. "I miss being able to talk to him. I feel like I'm the one dying." Finally she looked at me, her expression weary and pleading. "I wish God would just tell me what to do."

In the right circumstances, modern critical care saves lives. The moments when I have lifted my most raw and heartfelt praise to the Lord have occurred within the walls of the intensive care unit, when I have witnessed his grace and mercy made manifest in the recovery of a child battling a widespread infection, a man fighting for his life after a motorcycle crash, or a woman whose heart strains in the throes of a heart attack.

Yet medical technology harbors a dark side. When an illness cannot be cured, aggressive interventions prolong dying, incur suffering, and rob us of our ability to speak with loved ones and with God in our final days. Ventilators steal both voice and consciousness. Resuscitation looks a lot like assault. In the ICU we often awake in panic and find ourselves physically strapped to a foreign bed, deprived of the familiarity and comfort of home. We clamber for air, only to find we have no freedom and no voice.

When our critically ill loved ones cannot speak to us, we wrestle with impossible decisions of whether to press on or to withhold treatment, all while we yearn to hear a beloved voice again. Like the wife holding my dying patient's hand, such dilemmas thrust us into grief, doubt, fear, anger, and even guilt as we struggle to reconcile a web of hospital instruments with a mother's voice, a father's laughter, or a child's smile. While we wrestle, concerns about faith also haunt us. Death is a profoundly spiritual event that rips from us the people we most cherish and pitches us into doubt about suffering, mercy, and the God whom we serve. *What is God's will?* we ask. *Why is God allowing my loved one to suffer? What does the Bible allow in this scenario?* Such questions tap into our deepest anguish, a pain that echoes from our origins as image bearers torn from God. Death is the wages of our fallenness, and the final enemy (Rom. 6:23; 1 Cor. 15:26). Even Christ wept in the face of death (John 11:35).

Yet when they deliver devastating news, too often physicians—and I include myself among the culpable—ignore these concerns and suggest chaplaincy services as a conciliatory afterthought. We focus solely on monitors and machines, and, in so doing, we transform death from a process directed heavenward to one steeped in nomenclature and obscurity. Percentages soothe little when we pine for hope. Medical terms offer no solace when the soul thirsts for God (Ps. 42:1–2). When it so heaps decisions of life and death upon us without a grounding in faith and Scripture, medicine casts us adrift, rudderless. We stumble forward under duress, without understanding how the lines, tubes, and numbers equate with the truth that "death has been swallowed up in victory" through Christ (1 Cor. 15:54).

The idea for this book arose in my heart during my ten years caring for patients in the intensive care unit (ICU), first during my surgical and critical care training and then as a trauma surgeon who worked extensively in the surgical ICU. Over the course of that decade, I had the privilege of partnering with people during their most vulnerable moments, and I loathed the disconnect between the technical details that I laid out and the pain tearing them apart. As I would lean forward in my white coat to inquire about resuscitation and feeding tubes, the weight of unvoiced questions bore down upon us—questions of God's authority, of his goodness, of sanctity of life, and of suffering. These questions sprang from concerns fundamental to our Christian faith, but they hid beneath the trappings and decorum of a secular medical system.

To honor God in the bleak setting of the ICU, we must clarify the expanse between life and death that our medical advances have blurred. The shift of dying from the home to the hospital challenges us to acknowledge the capabilities and limitations of the technology upon which we lean, and to embrace it in a fashion that keeps the gospel in focus. Compassionate, gospel-centered guidance in end-of-life care requires a consideration of medical technology through the lens of heaven. We must unravel the jargon and the statistics and appraise them against the clarifying light of the Word.

When I speak of "life-prolonging," "life-sustaining," or "organ-supporting" technology, I refer to the array of medical interventions that augment or replace failing organ systems, e.g., ventilators for failing lungs, and dialysis for failing kidneys. Doctors usually implement such measures in emergency or ICU settings, when organ failure is life threatening. The introductory chapters of this book provide a framework for understanding such treatment in broad brushstrokes, coupled with a discussion of the biblical principles that undergird Christian medical ethics. Thereafter, chapters focus on specific categories of life-sustaining technology. These discussions revolve around individual patient encounters and include in layman's terms candid explanations of the interventions, their limitations, and their curative potential.

I have changed identifying details, including gender and diagnosis, to protect the privacy of the patients and families who inspired this book. Additionally, in some places I have combined narratives into composite accounts to more effectively highlight key issues. Throughout, however, I have endeavored to preserve the rawness of the struggle that patients and families face as they navigate end-of-life dilemmas. In particular, the conversations are accurate, taken in many cases from my own notes over the years of encounters I dared not forget.

My hope is that through this book, Christian believers grappling with decisions about life-prolonging measures can confront their situation with peace and discernment. Although clergy and healthcare professionals will find *Between Life and Death* useful, I wrote it for patients and their loved ones as they face the unthinkable. If you are facing terminal illness or discussing end-of-life wishes with a physician, I recommend reading this book in its entirety. On the other hand, if the tempest of critical illness pressures you into urgent decision making, with little time to read and digest, I suggest reading the chapters "Framing the Issue" and "Wisdom Begins with the Word," and then referencing the sections pertaining to your specific situation. "Advance Care Planning" and "Being a Voice" will offer guidance in making decisions for yourself or your loved ones. Key points at the end of each chapter provide quick reference, and relevant resources, including a sample advance directive and suggested reading, appear in the appendices. Throughout, I have endeavored to write in plain language; however, I have included medical terminology in parentheses throughout the book, and definitions of these terms appear in the glossary.

I have no intention of dictating how to proceed clinically in every case. Any medical decisions should occur on an individual basis, in collaboration with a trusted doctor and with your unique attributes, values, and circumstances central to the discussion. Rather, I seek to inform, to decode the jargon, and to provide a biblical framework for key issues you may encounter in an ICU setting. I hope to provide clarity and solace to the son at the bedside, the grandmother weighing her options, and the patient whose life flickers and wanes before the life to come.

I never trained at a seminary. I write as a follower of Christ and a specialist in critical care who, after becoming a believer during her ICU training, found herself counseling patients and families through heart-wrenching dilemmas on a near-daily basis, and who found dialogue about medical choices in the context of Christian values glaringly absent. Mentors among pastors and ethicists kindly guided me in the writing of this book, and I am sincerely grateful for their insights.

As we delve into a shadowy realm, I pray for those of you struggling with the heart-wrenching dilemmas touched upon in these pages. I pray that whatever the outcome, the Lord may grant you strength and peace, even in the grim hours when life dwindles. In end-of-life care, the best answers are not about right or wrong but about God's grace, manifest in Christ (John 3:16). May we rest in the assurance that however total our heartbreak, and however devastating the path before us, God has triumphed over sin, his love for us surpasses understanding, and this broken world is not the end. As Paul writes, "Neither death nor life, nor angels nor rulers, nor things present nor things to come, nor powers, nor height nor depth, nor anything else in all creation, will be able to separate us from the love of God in Christ Jesus our Lord" (Rom. 8:38–39).

PART I

DYING, but ALIVE

in CHRIST

I

FRAMING *the* ISSUE

She reminded me of a sparrow buffeted by wind. Her diminutive frame trembled, and a nurse placed a hand on her back to steady her as she teetered beside her husband's bed.

Her husband watched through glazed eyes. His chest rose and fell with a sickly cadence, like that of a maimed bird beating its wings to take flight. He seemed remote, his mind wandering through forgotten country. He had developed pneumonia after a difficult surgery, and as infection clogged his lungs, delirium seized him. His bleary gaze searched a space none of us could see.

"He doesn't want it!" his wife insisted.

The surgeon drew nearer to her. "I don't think you understand me. He's already gotten through the surgery. He's made it this far. I think he would want the breathing tube."

"No, doctor, he wouldn't," she retorted, her voice cracking. "We talked about this so many times, and he was crystal clear. He's always said, 'When God calls me home, let me go.'"

The surgeon folded his arms. "But how can you be so sure that God is calling him home right now? You realize he'll die without the tube, right?"

Her face reddened. She opened her mouth to speak, but for several moments words failed her. Veins swelled in her neck. "No tube!" she finally managed.

The nurse's eyes met mine, and she pleaded with me to intervene. I urged the surgeon to allow me to speak with the patient's wife in private.

"Please, help her to understand," he urged me as he left the room. He shook his head as he walked toward the ICU double doors.

I sat beside my patient's wife and cupped one of her hands in my own. With her free hand, she clutched her husband's fingers. In contrast with her broken spirit, her grasp seemed forged from iron.

"Please," I ventured, "can you tell me about your husband? What is he like?"

A thin smile graced her face, and her demeanor softened. She described for me their sixty-year marriage, the partnership they shared, the tenderness, the trust. She outlined his declining health over the last year and his inability to engage in the things that set his mind and heart afire. Pain, immobility, and shortness of breath confined him to the house. Visits with friends, once life giving, now exhausted him. The fog of pain and medication so clouded his thinking that he could no longer concentrate long enough to read, not even to skim the Bible that sat on his bedside and which for decades had steered him through tempests. His own father had suffered a slow, painful death in the ICU, and he had pleaded with her to shield him from the interventions he witnessed. The very idea of a ventilator horrified him.

"He didn't even want this surgery," she related to me. "I persuaded him to go through with it because I wasn't ready to give up time with him. On the way to the hospital, he made me promise I'd say no to tubes or CPR or anything like that. He couldn't stand the thought of it. He's always said, 'Let me go home to God.'" Her voice cracked again. "He's going through all this out of love for me. The breathing machine would be too much."

I squeezed her hand. "I think he's made the decision for us."

Afterward, we reinstated the do-not-intubate order that he had established prior to surgery.[1] His breathing would fail without a ventilator, but to force him onto one against his wishes, when its efficacy was dubious and his suffering certain, lacked all semblance of compassion. We changed our focus from cure to comfort. His surgeon, although disappointed, understood.

His nurse remained at his side around the clock to provide medication to alleviate pain and anxiety. When I left the ICU that evening, his wife rested beside him with her head in his lap. Although his gaze remained distant, he stroked her arm with his hand.

The following morning, I again found his wife in tears. Overnight their son had rushed to the hospital in a rage over the decision against a breathing tube.

"You're not going to kill my father!" he had bellowed at the staff. "I know my dad. He was a God-fearing man who until six months ago went to church every single Sunday. He would *not* be okay with this." He threatened to call the police before he stormed out.

When I entered, I found the patient's wife crumpled and broken at her husband's bedside, his hand still clasped in her own.

"Doctor, I don't want to upset anyone," she said. "Maybe I'm not supposed to argue about this, and just do what everyone else says. But I *promised* him. I know he wants to go when God calls him. He trusts in God, not in all these machines. What else am I supposed to do?"

A Foreign Landscape

As dramatic as it may appear, the turmoil this family endured occurs commonly in our era of intensive-care medicine. Next of kin find themselves in the unfathomable position of advocating for their loved ones in a foreign environment, complete with an undecipherable vocabulary. Among themselves, families bicker and disagree. Nurses fight tears as their patients grimace with yet another turn, yet another dressing change, yet another needle stick. At the center, heavy within the room but often unspoken, is the question of how faith informs the heart-wrenching, convoluted process. Openly, healthcare practitioners, patients, and families debate about prognosis, percentages, and advance directives. Inwardly, we all cry, *How long, O LORD?* (Ps. 13:1)

The tumult seems incongruous with our vision of life's end. For centuries, Western culture has conversed about death in euphemisms and poetry. We all long to "go gentle into that good night,"[2] and "to die, to sleep.[3]" We soften the vulgarity of death with the phrase "pass away," as if life were a gauzy breeze, a zephyr that pirouettes in the air before vanishing into silence. Literature, philosophy, politics, and next-door neighbors depict death as a subdued stepping over a threshold, replete with quiet resignation, as subtle as a passing whisper.

Even while we cling to such metaphors, the landscape has shifted beneath us. In 1908, 86 percent of people in the United States spent their final days at home, among family and cherished friends, in the spaces that forged their memories.[4] The particulars of dying reflected its spiritual reality as a passage from captivity to sin to renewal in Christ. It was profoundly personal and relational.

A century later, Americans still treasure this understanding of death and cite the home as its rightful domain. Over 70 percent of us in the United States wish to spend our final days as our predecessors did—at home, among those we love.[5] Yet in our era, *only 20 percent do.*[6] Death has passed from the purview of families, pastors, and the quiet of home to sterile rooms that resound with alarms. The majority of us now die in institutions, facilities that run the gamut from nursing homes to acute-care centers. Up to 25 percent of people over the age of sixty-five years spend their final days in an ICU, far removed from adored friends and glimmers of the past.[7]

Medical progress over the last fifty years has equipped doctors with technologies that, under the right circumstances, can save lives but also transmute death from a finite event into a prolonged and painful process. Death now commonly occurs in fits and starts, in a slow, confusing fragmentation of a life. It occurs within institutions, among medical personnel, distant from the view of families and the consolation of home. When technology so degrades a natural event into a complicated ordeal, our comprehension falters. Poetic constructs, while they appeal to our hearts, break down when death involves a mechanical ventilator, chest compressions, and feeding tubes. Even as Christians, we strive to understand how the numbers and equipment reconcile with the truth that "my flesh and my heart may fail, but God is the strength of my heart and my portion forever" (Ps. 73:26). God's perfect timing seems less distinct when machinery blurs the boundaries of life and death. His will may seem elusive to us when decisions about ventilators and resuscitation confront us with check boxes. We embrace an understanding of death rooted in hope—in the gospel—that does not align with the distressing decisions that subsume our final moments.

An Unsettling Silence

The transition of death from the home to the hospital hides the realities of dying from an entire culture. As time passes, those of us who know death before it strikes us personally shrink in number. Our fear of dying, already inherent, deepens when it lurks beneath the unfamiliar. Even physicians admit to avoiding discussions about end-of-life care with their patients, out of concern for inciting emotional distress.[8] The topic unsettles, and so few of us openly discuss our final days. We prefer to displace the issue from our minds until the need arises.

Unfortunately, most of us will be unable to articulate our wishes when the time comes, let alone prayerfully consider God's will. Severe illness frequently alters consciousness, creating delirium and encephalopathy that render us disoriented, paranoid, and even hallucinating. The silicone tube required for support on a mechanical ventilator obstructs the vocal cords, eliminating the ability to speak. To tolerate a tube within the airway, we require sedating medication, which inhibits even nonverbal communication. In addition to enshrouding sufferers in confusion, critical care deprives us of a voice.

When trepidation disallows us to discuss our mortality ahead of time, we strand those we love with impossible decisions. In a recent national survey, only 26.3 percent of adult respondents had completed an advance directive, i.e., a document to guide treatment preferences when we cannot speak for ourselves.[9] When doctors cannot communicate directly with us, and we have no advance directive to guide them, they will seek out our healthcare proxy or next of kin for management decisions. Yet many family members and friends feel ill-equipped for this role. The same fears that prevent us from talking openly about death obscure our wishes from those who eventually make hard choices for us.

Even when we complete an advance directive, such documents often oversimplify the realities of end-of-life care.[10] Standard forms reduce complex and highly nuanced issues to a series of check boxes. They require us to project our thoughts into the future concerning subjects about which we have little knowledge, and to pass judgments using a polarizing metric without middle ground. We declare on such forms that either we will accept a mechanical ventilator, or we will not. We indicate we will accept chest compressions, or we will not. Such a stark, concrete approach disregards the messy realities of intensive care, a field that abounds with caveats. If you have declared "no ventilator" on an advance directive form, would you refuse such an intervention for a completely reversible event? What if you require a ventilator for only twenty-four hours? What if support lasts two weeks, but afterward you can recover and return home? A check box can scarcely delineate such subtleties. The efficacy of an advance directive hinges upon the conversation with your physician during its completion and explicit documentation of your values, not upon the form itself.

The Value of Discernment

When we have not communicated our wishes about life-sustaining measures, family members have little to guide them. From the doorway of a hospital room, a patient who will recover may appear identical to one fighting for his life. In both scenarios, we may require a mechanical ventilator to breathe, and sedating medications may plunge us into unconsciousness. An array of poles with intravenous (IV) bags and pumps will surround us. Wires from monitors may coil from our chest and scalp. For the aggrieved spouse at the bedside, such foreign trappings render looming death indistinguishable from steady recovery.

Differentiating between life-threatening illness and self-limited conditions that require only transient support involves an educated interpretation of numbers: the ventilator settings, medication dosages, laboratory values, radiography studies, and vital signs. The specific disease processes at work, and their treatability, are paramount. Understanding requires, at minimum, a detailed discussion with a physician who is adept at translating the numbers and statistics into laymen's terms and can frame the situation into a picture that families can comprehend.

Unfortunately, experience communicating with clinicians can vary. Physicians without a background in palliative care report discomfort in discussing end-of-life issues and cite concerns over unclear prognosis, time constraints, patient emotional distress, and inadequate training as factors inhibiting such encounters. In acute scenarios, we must place immediate trust in a physician with whom we have no prior bond. Studies show that during such situations, doctors are more likely to pursue aggressive treatments that may not align with our wishes.[11] One in ten Medicare decedents have surgery during their last week of life, despite the fact that only 10 percent wish to spend their last days in the hospital.[12]

When unfamiliar medical details muddy understanding, we need to lean ardently upon our assurance in Christ. Yet in one study of the dynamics between physicians and the loved ones of dying patients, only 20 percent of discussions touched upon spirituality, despite the fact that 77.6 percent of surrogate decision makers reported faith as important to them.[13] In this same study, loved ones raised the topic of spirituality in the majority of cases, and in only 20 percent of these instances did physicians inquire further. Surveys with physicians and nurses suggest that although most value the spiritual needs of their patients at the end of life, few feel comfortable engaging in conversations about faith.[14] Healthcare practitioners report inadequate preparation for spiritual dialogues and suggest that such conversations fall outside their scope of practice.[15]

Thus, despite their currency in the most fundamental of spiritual issues—life and death—modern medical systems offer scant context for a faithful response. Meanwhile, faith directly informs the care we pursue. Research shows that those of us who report significant support from a religious community are less likely to receive hospice services, more likely to pursue aggressive interventions at the end of life, and more likely to die in the ICU.[16] The confusion—and anguish—of end-of-life care deepens when we divorce the technicalities of dying from its spiritual origins.

In the case scenario at the start of this chapter, Christian faith informed the perspectives of my patient's wife and son, yet they arrived at diametrically opposed conclusions. According to his wife, aggressive measures repulsed my patient because he wholeheartedly accepted God's authority over his life and death, and he saw his worsening physical and cognitive impairments as hindrances to a life of faith. His son, however, reasoned that his devotion to God would compel him to pursue every intervention possible to extend his life.

To provide compassionate, gospel-centered care at the end of life, we must tease apart both the theology and the medical insight that fuel such discrepancies. Dogmatic responses usually worsen confusion and heartbreak and dismiss conflicts that strike to the core of our faith. Our priorities run deep. In this disconcerting era that blurs the boundaries between life and death, we must strive always to respond with love and mercy, and to walk humbly with our God (Mic. 6:8). In the following chapter, we embark upon our journey through an exploration of God's Word.

Take-Home Points

- Although the majority of Americans would prefer to die at home, only 20 percent of us do. Most of us now die in institutions, and many in the intensive care unit.

- The changing landscape of death places us and our loved ones into heart-wrenching situations when we must make decisions about advanced medical options that we do not understand.

- Life-prolonging technology robs us of the ability to communicate, and few of us outline our wishes regarding end-of-life treatment before catastrophe strikes.

- Life-sustaining measures can save life, but when administered indiscriminately they can prolong suffering and death without benefit.

- Although our Christian faith is central to our approach to death, healthcare practitioners rarely offer spiritual support.

- A gospel-centered response to end-of-life critical care mandates consideration of the Word and acknowledgment of the potential benefits and limitations of intensive-care technology.

2

WISDOM BEGINS
with the WORD

When catastrophe strikes, the Bible offers hope and steadies the ground beneath us. It provides "a lamp to my feet and a light to my path" (Ps. 119:105). Against the dizzying clamor of the ICU, the Bible offers clarity and steadfastness. "The sum of your word is truth, and every one of your righteous rules endures forever" (Ps. 119:160). Our pursuit of a Christ-centered, God-honoring approach to end-of-life care begins with faithfulness to God and his Word.

In this chapter, we explore biblical tenets to guide us as we navigate end-of-life dilemmas. We will unpack Scripture as it relates to life, death, and suffering, with the aim of illuminating God's will amidst the sighing of ventilators and the clang of alarms. The precepts discussed here serve as a foundation for the ensuing chapters on life-sustaining technology.

Christian theology informs modern medical ethics, and so the principles outlined here may align with the recommendations of physicians. However, as mentioned in the previous chapter, doctors rarely attend to spiritual concerns. Furthermore, autonomy—

the principle of self-determination—assumes primary importance in secular medical ethics, while the Christian worldview steers away from rugged individualism in pursuit of God-honoring service, as we see from Paul's first letter to the church at Corinth: "Do you not know that your body is a temple of the Holy Spirit within you, whom you have from God? You are not your own, for you were bought with a price. So glorify God in your body" (1 Cor. 6:19–20). As Christians, we live not for ourselves but for the Lord (Col. 3:17). As we consider end-of-life care, our goals do not begin and end with our own worldly desires, but instead reflect our identity in Christ (Eph. 1:5; 2:19; 4:24). When confusion arises, I would encourage patients and families to seek counsel with a trusted member of the clergy. Resources in bioethics also appear in the bibliography at the end of this book, and may help.

Four Fundamental Precepts

An approach to critical care medicine through a Christian lens mandates reflection upon four key principles:[1]

1. Sanctity of mortal life
2. God's authority over life and death
3. Mercy and compassion
4. Hope in Christ

Tension between these fundamentals often incites confusion. In the clinical vignette in the previous chapter, for example, the patient's wife voiced acceptance of God's authority in her husband's death, while his son clung fiercely to the sanctity of life. As this case demonstrates, overemphasis of one concept to the exclusion of others often oversimplifies highly nuanced situations in the ICU and, in my experience, worsens suffering. Myriad well-meaning people have inadvertently committed loved ones to burdensome but futile interventions, and a protracted and painful death, for the sake of dogma. The complexities of intensive care, and the boundaries it blurs, do not accommodate undiscerning approaches. To honor God through end-of-life care, we must acknowledge the dynamic interplay of each of the following principles.

1. Sanctity of Mortal Life

Christian opposition to such highly politicized issues as abortion and the "right to die" movement derives—appropriately—from the view of mortal life as a sacred gift from God. As the author of the world, God "gives to all mankind life and breath and everything" (Acts 17:25). As beings created in God's image, we each possess God-given and irrevocable dignity. Our created origin as image bearers establishes our worth and potential:

> Then God said, "Let us make man in our image, after our likeness. And let them have dominion over the fish of the sea and over the birds of the heavens and over the livestock and over all the earth and over every creeping thing that creeps on the earth." (Gen. 1:26)

The psalmist writes, "You formed my inward parts; you knitted me together in my mother's womb. I praise you, for I am fearfully and wonderfully made" (Ps. 139:13–14). Furthermore, our worth is magnified in the incarnation: God became true man, dwelt among us, then died and rose for the forgiveness of sins, salvation, and eternal life (John 1:1, 14).

The Lord entrusts us with life and commands us to cherish it through the commandment, "You shall not murder" (Ex. 20:13). He grants us this sacred gift for a unique and exalted purpose, namely, to glorify him through stewardship of his creation: "Whether you eat or drink, or whatever you do, do all to the glory of God" (1 Cor. 10:31). Peter reminds us, "As each has received a gift, use it to serve one another, as good stewards of God's varied grace" (1 Pet. 4:10). Paul further elaborates in his letter to the Romans: "For if we live, we live to the Lord; and if we die, we die to the Lord. So then, whether we live or whether we die, we are the Lord's" (Rom. 14:8).

Such verses illuminate our call to treasure the life God has granted us and in everything to strive to glorify him. The sanctity of mortal life mandates that we advocate for the unborn and safeguard against physician-assisted suicide (see chapter 11). It also requires that when struggling with an array of decisions in the ICU, *we consider treatments with the reasonable potential to cure.*

Yet difficulties arise when patients and loved ones interpret "sanctity of life" to mean "do everything at all costs." When a disease process is reversible, and "everything" translates into measures that promise recovery, such an approach preserves life. However, the specifics of critical care are usually far murkier. What if an intervention cannot promise recovery at all? What if it offers a minimal chance for improvement but guarantees prolonged suffering? In circumstances when an intervention cannot promise cure, a "do everything" approach may prolong dying and risk harm through ineffective treatments.

Research suggests that those with high "religious coping"— i.e., those who depend upon faith to guide their decisions—seek more aggressive care at the end of life, even in the setting of terminal cancer.[2] In my experience, such pursuit often stems from a well-intended yet indiscriminately applied conviction about the sanctity of life. "I understand he won't get better," one aggrieved son declared to me, as we discussed care for his dying father, "but I believe in the God of the Bible, and the Bible says killing is wrong. The way I see it, if we stop everything, we're killing him. And I can't do that." Hours later, as we battered his father with chest compressions and jolts of electricity to keep him alive, his son pushed through the crowd of frantic clinicians with tears welling in his eyes. "Stop!" he shouted. "Just stop. It's enough. He's had enough."

As future chapters will elucidate, organ-supporting technology inflicts suffering *and does not necessarily effect cure.* The capability of a medical intervention to save life depends upon a host of specific factors, with disease process being paramount among them. An indiscriminate, dogmatic approach to life-sustaining interventions threatens to inflict harm upon the very people we seek to protect. We must be so careful. As we endeavor to preserve life that God himself crafted, we must acknowledge when our efforts prolong not life but rather a painful death.

2. God's Authority over Life and Death

Although Scripture describes death as the "last enemy" (1 Cor. 15:26), and although the thought if it may fill us with fear and dread, death persists in this earthly kingdom as the consequence of the fall. "The wages of sin is death" (Rom. 6:23), and it overtakes us all. "Sin came into the world through one man, and death through sin, and so death spread to all men because all sinned" (Rom. 5:12). Even Christ, who defeated death, first endured dying in submission to the Father (Matt. 26:36–45).

Although God directs us to honor the life he has created, he also reminds us of its fleeting nature. Like the grass of the fields, we are here today and gone tomorrow. Even long lives, humanly speaking, span a mere handbreadth from God's perspective (Ps. 39:5). *Sanctity of life does not refute the certainty of death.*

By his authority and Word, God is at work in all things, even death. Herod hastened his own death when he brought divine judgment upon himself for his impiety: "An angel of the Lord struck him down, because he did not give God the glory, and he was eaten by worms and breathed his last" (Acts 12:23). In contrast, King David, a man after God's own heart (1 Sam. 13:14), enjoyed a long life before succumbing to the ravages of old age (1 Chron. 29:28). Such texts do not, by any means, suggest the simplistic theology of Job's miserable comforters, who reduce death and suffering to a retributional, penalty-rewards system.

Death does not necessarily follow as punishment for specific sins (Job 20:27–29; 42:7). Rather, such texts reveal that the Lord *engages* with us, even as we draw our last breath, to effect good. From the first book of Samuel: "He brings down to Sheol and raises up" (1 Sam. 2:6). Per the psalmist: "You return man to dust, and say, 'Return, O children of man!'" (Ps. 90:3). Christ reanimated Lazarus from death so that his disciples would see and know by faith alone that he is the resurrection and the life (John 11). In the most breathtaking example, God gave his Son over to death, then raised him again for the forgiveness of sins, salvation, and eternal life.

When faced with the grief and uncertainty of life-threatening disease, fear may drive us to resist death at all costs. We may chase after aggressive interventions even when such measures promise no recovery. Yet when we so blind ourselves to our mortality, we deny the resurrection. We ignore that our times are in his hands (Ps. 31:15) and dismiss the power of his grace in our lives. We disregard the truth that the Lord works through all things—even death—for the good of those who love him (Rom. 8:28).

Christ's submission to the will of the Father can guide us. The Bible teaches that in the garden of Gethsemane, fear and despair seized Jesus as he anticipated his imminent death and the crushing abandonment he would endure for us on the cross (Matt. 27:46; see also Ps. 22:1; Heb. 12:1–3). "My soul is very sorrowful, even to death," he lamented to the disciples (Matt. 26:38). He knew his Father wielded the power to rescue him and so pleaded with him for mercy, yet he accepted God's will. "My Father, if it be possible, let this cup pass from me," he prayed with his face to the ground. "Nevertheless, not as I will, but as you will" (Matt. 26:39). Even on the cross, while onlookers jeered and provoked him, Christ remained faithful in his submission to the Father: "Like a lamb that is led to the slaughter, and like a sheep that before its shearers is silent, so he opened not his mouth" (Isa. 53:7).

When we confront critical illness, faith embraces and holds fast to this same spirit of acceptance and trust. God can perform miracles. Mountains melt before him, and he halts the sea in its landward charge (Ps. 97:5; Job 38:8–11). *Yet the miracles that would fulfill our most desperate longing may not align with his divine and perfect will.* As an example, the book of Job illustrates vividly how our own suffering can glorify God in ways hidden from our sight and understanding. After a long and heart-wrenching dialogue while in the depths of grief, Job relents to God in humility: "I know that you can do all things, and that no purpose of yours can be thwarted. . . . I have uttered what I did not understand, things too wonderful for me, which I did not know" (Job 42:2–3).

When deluged with fear and despair, we cling to our faith in the Lord's goodness and in his power to accomplish the unfathomable. Yet we must never convince ourselves that if we pray fervently enough, he must necessarily yield to *our* will. "Your will be done," we recite in the Lord's Prayer, as Jesus himself also prayed in the garden of Gethsemane (Matt. 6:10; 26:42). Over the years, I have watched numerous patients linger on machines days past the point of hope, as loved ones insist we continue all treatments and wait for God to intervene. "I know he's dying," one daughter declared to me. "But you need to keep the ventilator going. I'm praying for a miracle."

While we should pursue medical therapies with promise of cure, we err when we fight in the face of futility, stalwart in our belief that God will use technology to perform a miracle. Although we can empathize with these sentiments, especially during the heartbreak of sudden critical illness, such statements ignore God's authority. The Lord does not need a ventilator to save a life. Christ resurrected Lazarus with a word (John 11:43–44). He revived a dead girl with a touch of his hand (Luke 8:52–56). While the Lord has blessed us with medical advancements to combat death, their efficacy depends on his *mercy*. He does not need our help, nor does he call us to pursue futile interventions to give him time (Acts 17:24–25). When despondency and jargon befuddle us, we must diligently place our trust not in our own meager technology, but in the Lord's benevolence and power over death. To cling to interventions in the face of futility is to chase after idols. We worship the technology rather than its Creator.

3. Mercy and Compassion

God calls us to love our neighbors as ourselves (Matt. 22:39). "A new commandment I give to you, that you love one another: just as I have loved you, you also are to love one another" (John 13:34). Christ taught that service to God requires ministry to the downtrodden and afflicted. "By this we know love, that he laid down his life for us, and we ought to lay down our lives for the brothers. But if anyone has the world's goods and sees his brother in need, yet closes his heart against him, how does God's love abide in him?" (1 John 3:16–17). "Be merciful, even as your Father is merciful" (Luke 6:36). Christ's sacrifice inspired his apostles to call for compassion toward one another: "All of you, have unity of mind, sympathy, brotherly love, a tender heart, and a humble mind" (1 Pet. 3:8). "Beloved, if God so loved us, we also ought to love one another" (1 John 4:11). "Therefore be imitators of God, as beloved children. And walk in love, as Christ loved us and gave himself up for us, a fragrant offering and sacrifice to God" (Eph. 5:1–2). As God so loved us, as followers of Christ we must also extend ourselves in empathy and mercy toward one another.

Loving one another at the ICU bedside requires attention to suffering. When we inflict distress and pain upon one another unnecessarily, we fail in our mandate to love our neighbor, even when we pursue such measures with good intent. Mercy does not justify active euthanasia or physician-assisted suicide (chapter 11). However, it does guide us away from aggressive, painful interventions if such measures are *futile*, or *if the torment they inflict exceeds the anticipated benefit*. The experience of suffering varies between individual people; what constitutes unacceptable hardship for you may not trouble me. A compassionate approach requires acknowledgment of subjective and individual constructs of suffering and a response infused with empathy.

Likewise, as we consider our own circumstances at the end of life, we are not obligated to pursue treatments that threaten our ability to serve God faithfully. As his image bearers, God grants us dignity and free will in our lives, with the expectations that our choices *aim to glorify him*. Long life is a blessing but not the ultimate good (1 Kings 3:10–14); richness in life springs from godly service, prayer, and worship (Ps. 19:10; 1 Cor. 11:23–26). God's Word does not require us to endure suffering to extend life if we cannot direct that extra time *toward faithful service to him*. Paul illustrates this point in contemplations of his own suffering and death, in his letter to the Philippians:

> For to me, to live is Christ, and to die is gain. If I am to live in the flesh, that means fruitful labor for me. Yet which I shall choose I cannot tell. I am hard pressed between the two. My desire is to depart and be with Christ, for that is far better. But to remain in the flesh is more necessary on your account. Convinced of this, I know that I will remain and continue with you all, for your progress and joy in faith, so that in me you may have ample cause to glory in Christ Jesus, because of my coming to you again. (Phil 1:21–26)

Paul was well acquainted with physical suffering (2 Cor. 12:7). In his letter to the Philippians, he reasons that prolonged life in the midst of suffering is a greater good, only if it continues *in service to God*. While he longs to be with Christ, he presses on so that he may encourage believers in their walk with the Spirit. Our ability to serve God faithfully, then, influences our choices as we consider end-of-life care. We need not pursue life-prolonging treatments if they strip us of our capacity to live for the Lord.

4. Hope in Christ

As Christians, we rest in a hope without equal: "According to his great mercy, he has caused us to be born again to a living hope through the resurrection of Jesus Christ from the dead, to an inheritance that is imperishable, undefiled, and unfading, kept in heaven for you" (1 Pet. 1:3–4). God's love for us endures even in our final moments on earth: "Even though I walk through the valley of the shadow of death, I will fear no evil, for you are with me" (Ps. 23:4). We rejoice that through Christ's resurrection, "death is swallowed up in victory" (1 Cor. 15:54–55). So vast is God's love for us, so breathtakingly superb his sacrifice, that nothing can pry us from him (Rom. 8:38–39). Even as we suffer, we rejoice in the news that Christ has relinquished us from the permanence of death. We savor the promise of the resurrection of the body and the hope of eternal union with God. From Paul's first letter to the Thessalonians, "since we believe that Jesus died and rose again, even so, through Jesus, God will bring with him those who have fallen asleep" (1 Thess. 4:14).

The saving gospel of Jesus Christ transforms our view of dying. Even as we wrestle with decisions about ventilators and chest compressions, and even as we consider our final moments, we need not fear death! "For this light momentary affliction is preparing us for an eternal weight of glory beyond all comparison, as we look not to the things that are seen but to the things that are unseen" (2 Cor. 4:17–18). Christ has vanquished sin. Through the gospel, fear of our transient earthly death withers before the assurance of renewed life. As Christians, we share an immaculate hope unrivaled by any in human history. We rest assured of Christ's promise by faith alone: "Whoever believes in me, though he die, yet shall he live, and everyone who lives and believes in me shall never die" (John 11:25–26). Christ's resurrection transforms death from an event to be feared into an instrument of God's grace as he calls us home to heaven. Although we die, we are alive in Christ.

Preservation of Life versus Prolongation of Death

To summarize, a gospel-centered approach to end-of-life care hinges upon the principles of sanctity of life, God's authority over death, mercy, and hope in Christ. In concert, these tenets guide us to seek cure, but also to accept death when it arrives and to alleviate suffering when possible. Distinguishing between these elements—which appear stark on paper, but tangled and messy at the bedside—depends upon a key question: "Will life support in this scenario constitute *preservation of life* or *prolongation of death and undue suffering?*"

Medical technology, while sophisticated, is imperfect. Life-sustaining measures are *supportive*, not curative. Doctors force air into the lungs, constrict blood vessels with potent drugs, filter the blood when kidneys fail, compel the heart to pump harder, and in experimental cases even bypass liver function, but none of these maneuvers cures disease. They only buy time.

Life-sustaining treatment intends to buoy organ function long enough to correct the underlying illness. Physicians use such techniques to support us while they manage our widespread infection, occluded heart vessels, or stroke. If the inciting disease is treatable, then life support is indeed "life-saving," because it maintains our body systems long enough for us to recover. However, if the core illness is irreversible, life support prolongs our dying without benefit.

Why should we avoid prolongation of death? As previously outlined, God calls us to love our neighbors and to minister to the suffering. Life-sustaining technology *inflicts suffering*. Patients who survive critical illness report high rates of post-traumatic stress disorder (PTSD).[3] Cardiopulmonary resuscitation (CPR), the chest compression technique that medical professionals perform with solemnity and television actors with bravado, breaks ribs.[4] Patients undergoing mechanical ventilation report panic, anxiety, and fear of suffocation. Prolonged bed restriction breaks down skin, freezes joints, and induces pain with simple repositioning.

Hope for recovery, with resultant preservation of life, warrants such extreme measures. Without expectation for improvement, however, these interventions constitute cruelty. Our challenge is to decipher when medical treatment has crossed the threshold from life saving, to death prolonging.

Inviting Christ to the Bedside

How does one weave these principles into the narrative of a loved one clinging to life? How do we deconstruct the lines and tubes and demystify the infusion pumps and the hum of continuous dialysis? How do we frame our own grief and desperation within the context of the gospel of Jesus Christ, our refuge and strength (Ps. 46:1)?

Few physicians will volunteer for a spiritual dialogue. However, asking a medical care team specific, focused questions can illuminate where a condition falls along the spectrum between life and death. Armed with responses to these questions, as well as with biblical evidence of the sanctity of life, the value of mercy, and the inevitability of death, we can more clearly ascertain when the Lord urges us to press onward, or when he beckons us home:

- What is the condition that threatens my loved one's life?
- Why is the condition life threatening?
- What is the likelihood for recovery?
- How do my loved one's previous medical conditions influence his/her likelihood for recovery?
- Can the available treatments bring about cure?
- Will the available treatments worsen suffering, with little chance of benefit?
- What are the best and worst expected outcomes?

Answers to these questions may unveil the truth with painful clarity. Some conditions so devastate the body that the certainty of death is obvious to all. More frequently, however, a clinical course fluctuates. Families and practitioners alike should return to this inquiry frequently, as recovery or decline evolves over time. Furthermore, all should feel empowered to seek second opinions, should we distrust the assessment of a treating physician.

Paramount throughout end-of-life challenges is to couple contemplation with ardent prayer. Grief, anger, and anxiety flood both heart and mind during such ordeals and may obscure the path that God prepares for us. Compassion must galvanize our actions. When anguish and jargon disorient us, we must immerse ourselves in the Word of God, the Bible. Only then can we minister to one another and to those we love, when calamity ensnares us into an ICU.

Take-Home Points

- A biblical approach to end-of-life care mandates consideration of four principles:

  1. Sanctity of mortal life
  2. God's authority over life and death
  3. Mercy and compassion
  4. Hope in Christ

- Our life constitutes a gift from God, and our identity in Christ a call to glorify him in both our body and soul. We have a responsibility to preserve life when possible. We should consider accepting treatments that promise cure.

- Efforts to prolong life when there is limited hope of recovery threaten to prolong dying rather than save life, ignore God's authority over death, and discount our great hope and faithfulness in Christ.

- When aggressive measures inflict suffering upon patients, either in excess of anticipated medical benefits or in the case of clear futility, we fail in our mandate to love one another.

- Asking a treating medical team key questions about disease and recovery can guide us to determine if aggressive treatments offer hope of life, or prolonged suffering and death.

PART 2

A DETAILED LOOK at ORGAN-SUPPORTING MEASURES

3

RESUSCITATION for
CARDIAC ARREST

As we consider life-sustaining measures, it helps to categorize them into two classes:

1. Resuscitation. When death is imminent, physicians intervene to salvage life (e.g., with CPR).
2. Organ support. After initial resuscitation, organ support is continued in the ICU (e.g., with a mechanical ventilator).

Untangling Definitions

Overlap exists between these two categories, but this framework helps guide our thoughts as we consider end-of-life care. In this chapter, we will review the resuscitation phase, i.e., treatments offered acutely to save a life when death is imminent. The next chapter will provide an overview of organ support provided in the ICU.

Paramedics, physicians, or other first responders responding to 911 calls perform resuscitative maneuvers when we go into cardiac arrest or when we stop breathing. Doctors may also resuscitate us in the hospital. Here we will focus on cardiac arrest, specifically CPR (cardiopulmonary resuscitation) and defibrillation. Physicians often place a tube into the airway during CPR, but we will defer discussion about that until our review of mechanical ventilation in chapter 5. Additionally, we will examine do-not-resuscitate orders in chapter 12.

To begin, let us direct our attention past jargon and theory to the heart of the matter: the impact of cardiac arrest upon those who love, breathe, and yearn.

At the Bedside

He worked as an arborist until disseminated cancer snatched him from the treeline. When he retired his harness, dementia soon followed, and afternoons found him far from home, wandering in unfamiliar places and conversing with strangers.

During one such amble, he toppled down a flight of concrete stairs and lay bleeding on the pavement for half a day. A store clerk discovered him and called for help. When paramedics arrived, they could barely detect a pulse.

Upon arrival at the emergency department (ED), his faint pulse disappeared. A dozen doctors and nurses scrambled to revive him. They pushed on his chest, pumped him full of powerful medications, and guided a tube into his windpipe.

After half an hour, he regained a pulse but then lost it again. Several more rounds of CPR resumed. When his pulse finally returned, his blood pressure hovered precipitously low, and his heart rhythm convulsed in erratic beats. Laboratory tests revealed high levels of acid in his bloodstream, and failing kidneys. A computed tomography (CT) scan of his head showed a fractured skull and a large blood clot compressing his tumor-studded brain.

When I entered his room to examine him, his daughter watched me through a sheen of tears. She huddled in her chair with her arms wrapped around herself and caressed a gold cross between two fingers.

I rubbed his sternum, examined his head wound, and flashed a light in his eyes. His extremities were dusky and cool to the touch. Bruises blackened his skin. A high dose of medication dripped into his veins to constrict his blood vessels and shunt blood to his organs. As I watched the monitor, his heart tracing periodically spasmed into an ominous rhythm.

I sat down with her and searched her face. Love, conflict, and despair deepened in her eyes. "I'm so sorry for what's happened," I ventured. The words seemed shallow, a string of platitudes.

"I know it's bad," she replied. "He didn't want any this. None of it. The other doctors . . ." she motioned to the door of the room. "They did what they had to. They didn't know he was DNR."

"Wait—he had a do-not-resuscitate order?" Dread swept over me as I realized he had signed an order prohibiting the battery of invasive treatments he had just received.

"Yes."

"How clear was he about his wishes?"

"Before his mind started to go? He had a body full of cancer, and he knew it. He didn't want any of this. But now they've done everything, and they want me to be the one to say, 'stop.' How can I do that? How can I say, 'Don't save my father'? He's my dad. I love him."

When she spoke these last words, an alarm sounded, and his heart tracing flattened. We leapt in yet again with compressions and shouts and medications. As we performed CPR, his shoulders sprang off the stretcher with each thrust, with each grisly attempt to squeeze blood from his heart.

After ten minutes of CPR had still not achieved a pulse, she asked us to stop. Agony darkened her face. As the crowd of clinicians thinned from the room, and as I too exited with eyes downcast, I glimpsed her holding her head in her hands and weeping.

It's Not Like on TV

The emergency bay in which my treetop-seeking patient clung to life harbored no hint of excitement. As is so common when death looms, the air hung heavy with sorrow and yearning (Ps. 42:2). The loss of a life has a way of hollowing us out, of expunging all traces of hope.

Unfortunately, such realities defy the expectations promoted by popular media. Sitcoms portray cardiac arrest in moments thick with hyperbole, with nurses hollering for help and heroic doctors rushing in with paddles raised high. While such depictions capture the adrenaline of medical crises, they ignore the desperation and dread that seize all involved. They dismiss the brutality inherent to resuscitation and the remorse that troubles doctors and nurses who, as adherents to a profession built upon altruism, are paradoxically tasked with administering treatments that seem barbaric and futile. They disregard the turmoil thrust upon families as their loved ones linger between life and death, suspended in a place where God's will appears elusive.

In addition to trivializing the emotional upheaval that resuscitation stirs, television can wrongly skew confidence in CPR. Outcomes in the hospital differ starkly from the grand portrayals on TV.[1] Sitcoms depict a CPR survival rate *double* that which occurs in the real world.[2] Additionally, rarely do TV programs illustrate treatment limitations, and they ignore the effects of preexisting health conditions that significantly worsen CPR outcomes.[3]

Such inaccuracies mislead us. In one survey of patients over the age of seventy, the majority of whom cited television as their source of information, 81 percent estimated their chances of surviving CPR at 50 percent or better.[4] Twenty-three percent thought their chances of survival was as high as 90 percent. In reality, the survival rate after CPR is dismal. On average, *less than 10 percent* of patients who receive CPR leave the hospital alive.[5] Fallacious depictions of CPR in popular media are not only dishonest, but dangerous, because they lull us into false hope. They convince us to chase after brutal treatments even in futility.

To navigate issues of resuscitation with discernment, we must put down our smartphones. With faith in Christ motivating our quest, we must disregard hyperbole and examine the realities of cardiac arrest and resuscitation with clear vision. We must cast aside drama and consider reality with our minds and hearts fixed on the cross (Col. 3:17).

Introduction to Cardiac Arrest

The job of the heart is to pump blood throughout the body. Blood collects oxygen from small blood vessels in your lungs, and then the heart pumps this blood to your organs, to supply your cells with the oxygen they need to produce energy. Cardiac arrest occurs when this delivery system fails. Physicians commonly refer to cardiac arrest as the heart "stopping"; however, in most cases the heart actually continues to beat but does so ineffectively. When the heart cannot pump blood with enough strength to produce a pulse in the neck, oxygen deprivation damages cells within minutes. Without an adequate supply of oxygen, cells eventually deplete their energy reserves and die.

The speed and extent of cell injury in cardiac arrest depends on the organ in question. For example, skeletal muscle, like that in your arms and legs, can sustain lack of oxygen for as long as thirty minutes. In contrast, the needs of the brain are so high, and its energy reserves so limited, that without oxygen its cells suffer irreversible damage in just four to six minutes.[6] So vulnerable is the brain to low oxygen levels that cardiac arrest is associated with a high risk of brain damage, especially with any delay in CPR. If blood flow is not restored quickly after cardiac arrest, you suffer severe brain damage at best. If cardiac arrest cannot be reversed, death is inevitable.

Causes of Cardiac Arrest

The heart contains a network of electrical fibers, with a bundle between the upper (atrial) chambers coursing like a power cable toward the lower (ventricular) chambers. This bundle ensures the normal flow of blood to and from the heart.

In two-thirds of cardiac arrest cases, this electrical system in the heart misfires.[7] Electrical cells elsewhere in the heart can override command of the main bundle in severe disease, and when this happens the heart takes on a chaotic rhythm. In some cases, the heart muscle quivers, without coordination between chambers (ventricular fibrillation, or V-fib). In others, the ventricles pump too quickly to fill with blood (ventricular tachycardia, or V-tach). In the worst cases, electrical activity of the heart stops altogether (asystole). Any of these scenarios can produce cardiac arrest, i.e., loss of a pulse due to diminished blood flow throughout the body.

In the remaining cases of cardiac arrest, the heart beats with a normal rhythm, but disease or injury impedes delivery of blood to the organs. Trauma, massive bleeding, myocardial infarction ("heart attack"), and clot within the arteries of the lungs are common culprits.

Cardiopulmonary Resuscitation (CPR)

CPR refers to manual compression of the heart between the backbone and the breastbone. Clinicians place their hands on your chest and press down with their upper-body weight to squeeze your heart between your sternum and your spine. This maneuver mimics circulation and aims to maintain blood flow to the brain and heart until cardiac arrest can be reversed.

Contrary to popular perception, CPR does not *fix* cardiac arrest. Rather, it aims to provide oxygen to brain cells until doctors can correct the cause of cardiac arrest. In other words, CPR *buys time*.

In the event of a quickly reversible problem, CPR saves lives. Even outside the hospital, with only nonprofessional bystanders available to help, CPR increases the likelihood of survival from cardiac arrest threefold.[8] As a striking example, a young patient of mine fell unconscious in the ICU when his heart lapsed into a fatal rhythm (arrhythmia). After a minute of CPR and one shock with the defibrillator, he sat bolt upright in bed. With his face screwed into a befuddled expression, he scanned the hoard of clinicians staring at him and asked why his room was so crowded.

Such dramatic outcomes with CPR occur most commonly among healthy patients with a quickly fixable issue. More complicated circumstances, in contrast, should temper our enthusiasm. While essential for survival, CPR can inflict serious harm when employed indiscriminately.

After fifteen years, the memory of my first experience with CPR continues to haunt me. In a middle-of-the-night emergency as a medical student, I performed my first-ever round of compressions on an elderly woman whom I had never met. She appeared haggard, her muscles wasted away, her sunken temples betraying years of debilitating disease and malnutrition. Her lifeless eyes were fixed on the ceiling.

My hands trembled as I dutifully fell into the rhythm my instructors had taught me. On the first compression, I tried not to focus on her troubling and vacant stare. On the second, as I sank my weight into her breastbone, the dear lady's ribs cracked beneath my hands. The crunch of the bones flooded me with nausea. I fought the impulse to recoil, and squeezed my eyes shut to focus on the rhythm, the counting, and the protocol, rather than on the grotesqueness of each compression.

She regained a pulse after twenty minutes of resuscitation but sustained severe brain injury, as well as bruising and bleeding of her lungs from the CPR. She spent her last days unconscious, fighting a ventilator. When her family realized cure was impossible, they made the heart-wrenching decision to focus on her comfort and let her go.

Sadly, my introduction to CPR represents a disturbingly common scenario. Overall, only 30 to 50 percent of people who suffer cardiac arrest survive resuscitation, and only 6 to 15 percent live to leave the hospital.[9] Of the small number of us who survive, 34 to 50 percent will suffer brain injury from oxygen deprivation, with deficits ranging from mild memory impairment to severe disabilities in language, attention, and thinking (cognition).[10] Many of us who undergo CPR in the throes of severe illness will never return to our former selves.

In addition, skeletal chest injury, ranging from broken ribs to a fractured breastbone, occurs in up to 90 percent of people who undergo CPR.[11] As anyone who has sustained a rib fracture can attest, such trauma inflicts stabbing chest pain with each breath. Bones require immobilization to heal, yet ribs move every time we breathe. The recovery process is long and slow, and the simple act of breathing elicits pain.

When administered judiciously, CPR saves lives. However, when the chances of survival from cardiac arrest are low, CPR looks and feels like defilement rather than care. To make informed decisions about CPR, we must clarify prognosis and likely outcomes, taking into account our unique medical history and with the gospel guiding our way.

But before we plunge ahead, let us pause to explore the role of defibrillation in cardiac arrest.

External Defibrillation

External defibrillation refers to an electrical shock that resets the heart. This jolt of electricity is applied across the chest with paddles or pads, and it reverses abnormally chaotic heart rhythms (ventricular fibrillation) or rhythms that force the heart to contract too quickly (ventricular tachycardia). In each of these variations of cardiac arrest, defibrillation enables normal pacemaking cells of the heart to assume control again.

While TV scenes of doctors wielding paddles wax cartoonish, they *do* capture the crucial impact of defibrillation on survival. The odds of surviving cardiac arrest from an abnormal ventricular rhythm are *five times* higher than for other causes, precisely because of the power of defibrillation to help.[12] Approximately

25 to 40 percent of people who arrest from ventricular fibrillation survive to hospital discharge.[13] Patients with unstable ventricular tachycardia fare even better, with up to 65 to 70 percent leaving the hospital alive.[14] In contrast, only 2 to 11 percent of patients with cardiac arrest from other causes—e.g., complete interruption of electrical activity in the heart, bleeding, trauma, blood clots—live to return home.[15] This dramatic discrepancy highlights the potential of defibrillation to save life.

Defibrillation incurs little suffering. The region of the brain responsible for awareness requires tight regulation of blood flow, so in cardiac arrest, unconsciousness occurs instantly. While in other circumstances a jolt of electricity to the chest would inflict severe pain, in the case of cardiac arrest, we are unaware when paddles contact our skin. As with my young patient who awoke confused after a single shock, people who survive defibrillation rarely recall the event.

On the other hand, a similar procedure, electrical cardioversion, uses a lower voltage of electricity to treat abnormal heart rhythms less severe than those causing cardiac arrest. People who require cardioversion are usually awake, and those who require it rarely tolerate it without intravenous sedatives.

Putting It Together

Most of us will encounter decisions about cardiac arrest either in the calm of our primary care doctor's office or more urgently when it threatens a loved one in the emergency department or ICU. In all circumstances, candid, thorough discussions with a trusted physician are crucial. Our path requires careful review of the factors influencing survival and reflection upon Scripture to do as God requires: "to do justice, and to love kindness, and to walk humbly with your God" (Mic. 6:8). In short, we need to determine when to press on and when to relax into the embrace of our Lord.

A host of factors influence the likelihood that CPR will help. Abnormal ventricular rhythms, for example, confer better chances for survival than other causes. On the other hand, you are less likely to recover if you require CPR for longer than five to ten minutes, or if you have multiple episodes of arrest requiring repeated CPR. If you survive initial CPR, factors such as abnormally low blood pressure, persistent coma, need for a ventilator, pneumonia, and kidney failure still all decrease your chances of leaving the hospital. Details from your personal medical background also play a role, with the following conditions decreasing the chances for survival after cardiac arrest, even with prompt provision of CPR:[16]

- preexisting cancer
- Alzheimer's disease
- widespread infection (sepsis)
- severe stroke
- two or more chronic medical conditions (e.g., diabetes, hypertension, chronic kidney disease)
- heart disease, especially advanced congestive heart failure

I do not suggest, in listing these conditions, that everyone affected by them should decline CPR. Rather, I urge you to consider, prayerfully and in collaboration with a doctor, how your individual circumstances will influence the outcome of CPR. Diseases vary in severity. As unique, loved image bearers of God, we all differ in our rigor, strength, and resilience. If your unique medical story promises a high likelihood of recovery from cardiac arrest, then as a steward of God-given life, you should carefully consider accepting CPR. On the other hand, if significant medical illnesses already enfeeble you, dogged pursuit of resuscitation might only delay death and incur suffering.

To illustrate, let us return to the gentleman at the start of this chapter. He arrived in the emergency department with kidney failure and with a heart rhythm that defibrillation could not fix. He suffered from preexisting dementia and cancer, and required prolonged CPR. After he regained his pulse, he remained unresponsive, suggestive of brain injury and coma, and he also required medication to support a dangerously low blood pressure. With so many severe illnesses and injuries afflicting him, his recurrent cardiac arrest was unsurprising. His previous declaration of "do-not-resuscitate" reflected an accurate assessment of what CPR would mean for him.

While in retrospect, the futility of CPR in this gentleman's case appears clear, his daughter's uncertainty reflects a common conundrum in end-of-life care. In the quiet and calm of a doctor's office, decisions of aggressive care may seem obvious. When calamity strikes, however, the weight of guilt and grief bears down upon us, adding confusion and misery to an already heartbreaking scenario. In addition to the question of what our loved one would want, and how we will carry on without him or her, as Christians we also agonize over what God permits.

When aggressive care is futile, a gospel-centered response recognizes that our earthly lives end, that God works for good even in death, and that through Christ's resurrection, we belong to God. When we recognize that CPR will only inflict further harm, a view of the cross guides us to relinquish our grip on this world and commit our spirit into the hands of the Lord (Ps. 31:5; Luke 23:46).

Whether we cling to the glimmers of life or resign ourselves to the certain end of mortal life that awaits us, let us seek to glorify the one who knows us, who molded our bodies, and who so loves us that he gave his Son so we might also know resurrection and life everlasting (Psalm 139; John 3:16; 1 Cor. 6:19–20; 15:50–55). Even while death of the body looms, the Spirit endures. While we wait, we cling to the promise of the life to come: "I am the resurrection and the life. Whoever believes in me, though he die, yet shall he live" (John 11:25).

Take-Home Points

- Cardiac arrest refers to interruption of blood flow from the heart to the body, either by an abnormal rhythm, by a structural problem with the heart, or from a noncardiac cause such as bleeding or blood clot.

- Because the heart delivers oxygen to all parts of the body, cardiac arrest is lethal.

- CPR and defibrillation are the two key interventions in cardiac arrest. When used wisely, they can be life saving. When used indiscriminately, they prolong the dying process and incur unnecessary suffering at the end of life.

- Determination of whether CPR and defibrillation promise to save your life or incur suffering requires a meticulous review of your medical history with a trusted doctor.

4

INTRODUCTION to INTENSIVE CARE

After initial CPR, care for a critically ill person transitions to the ICU, where nurses and physicians provide meticulous monitoring and treatment using a wide array of technology. This chapter provides an overview of the purpose, promise, and limitations of ICU care.

We begin at the bedside.[1]

At the Bedside

When jaundice yellowed my patient's skin, her mother massaged her face and arms with jasmine lotion. When her eyes, vacant and bloodshot, darted about the room in delirium, photographs soon papered the walls, and favorite toys piled atop her. Daily her mother read *Harry Potter* aloud to her and recalled memories alive with the seashore and laughter.

Three months earlier she had entered the ICU doors with her abdomen swollen with infection. After a dozen surgeries, impenetrable scar encased her intestines. Over and over, she would creep forward a few steps toward recovery, and then an infection caused by our efforts to keep her alive would topple her backward. The ventilator gave her pneumonia. The catheters that delivered medications to maintain her blood pressure clotted and caused infection. All the while, the bacteria smoldering in her belly, never completely eradicated, released molecules into her bloodstream that made her blood vessels leak and her limbs balloon to elephantine proportions.

The day before my patient died, her mother crumpled into a hospital room chair and held her head in her hands. "She's not going to make it, is she?" she asked, without raising her head.

I didn't answer, but the weight of my hand on her shoulder conveyed my opinion. She quaked with grief beneath my palm. We sat in silence for a long while, she drawing deep breaths of lament, I subduing my own breaths, which seemed so intrusive against the tenderness of her anguish. "I keep begging God to take out my heart, to keep it from breaking," she finally whispered. "But I don't even know if he's listening anymore. My family says this happened to her because I stopped going to church. They say God's punishing me. *What if it's all my fault?*"

The next day, my patient spiked yet another fever, and her blood pressure plummeted. We had used every antibiotic in our arsenal, and a multidrug-resistant infection—a microbe we could not combat—had overtaken her. She required continuous dialysis for kidneys that would not recover. Her liver was failing. Contusions blotched her extremities as clotting factors in her blood unwound and drifted limply. While the ventilator still gave her breath, and medications still squeezed her blood vessels and stimulated her heart, our options to cure her had run out.

After a heart-wrenching discussion, her mother consented to discontinuing organ support. We would stop all medications, disconnect the ventilator, and focus on her comfort—and on saying goodbye.

At the end, her mother climbed into the hospital bed with her. She wrapped her arms around her and clutched her to herself, enfolding her in the same warmth she had offered to her as an infant. With tears streaming, she gripped her, prayed, and issued promises into her ear. As we witnessed a heart flayed open, all of us—nurses, doctors, students—cried along with her.

The Power to Support

Intensive care medicine has progressed dramatically since Florence Nightingale, the nurse who served during the Crimean War in 1850s Europe, first separated the most severely wounded soldiers from others for specialized care. This groundbreaking prioritization of the sickest patients progressed to "shock units" in World War II, then to iron lung wards for polio patients in the 1940s. With the advent of new techniques from 1988 to 2012, mortality among ICU patients dropped 35 percent.[2] Among people with chronic obstructive pulmonary disease, stroke, and heart attack, the survival benefits are even greater, with a 50 percent reduction in mortality.[3] Through the grace of God, we now have a vast array of interventions to support nearly every failing organ system. (The chart in appendix 1 outlines ICU measures in our arsenal and the organ systems they support.)

As a medical student I first witnessed the power of critical care to help. While on a rotation in pediatric surgery, I cared for a young boy whose abusive mother fractured his pancreas with a kick to the abdomen. In a matter of hours, his blood pressure declined, and his kidneys stopped making urine. His wide brown eyes disappeared as his eyelids swelled shut and his extremities ballooned. The pediatric intensivist and her team stood vigil at his bedside and fought to keep him alive until surgeons could take him to the operating room.

Two months later, I glimpsed him cavorting through the hallways of the main pediatric ward. A nurse ran after him, and he cast her a mischievous smile as he propelled himself forward on his IV pole as if it were a scooter. Aside from that IV pole, he resembled any other young child—frivolous, bursting with energy.

The machinery that had entangled him in the ICU helped restore him to himself.

Yet despite its promise, ICU care has limits. As we discussed in the previous chapter, cues from popular media tempt us to envision life-sustaining treatment in shades of melodrama. While rescues happen, a depressing number of ICU occupants follow the trajectory of the tragic girl in the opening scenario of this chapter. The longer we require life-sustaining measures, the more complications tally up. Eventually, our bodies wither and break down, until we can no longer combat the diseases eroding them.

Organ Support versus Cure

The inspiring story of the boy who recovered from his pancreatic injury illuminates an important point about ICU care. The ventilator and medications that ICU doctors determinedly implemented during his darkest hours did not actually *cure* him. They kept him alive, but his recovery hinged upon surgery for his torn pancreas. Without that operation, the inflammation ransacking his body would have killed him, regardless of the ventilator pushing air into his lungs. Similarly, despite weeks of the most intensive therapies ICU care offered, the young woman in the opening scenario died because we could not clear the infection from her abdomen. Her ultimate recovery depended not upon the ventilator but on our ability to manage the infection that brought her into the ICU in the first place.

This distinction between cure and support is critical. A ventilator cannot cure pneumonia. Cardiovascular medications cannot salvage dying heart muscle. Dialysis cannot kick-start the kidneys to function again. ICU measures like ventilators, vasopressor medications, and dialysis are *supportive, not curative.* They support failing organs until we can achieve a cure through other means—with antibiotics for pneumonia, a stent for a heart attack, or kidney transplantation for end-stage renal disease. Our ability to return a patient home depends upon our power to achieve *cure;*

ICU measures only support organ function in the meantime. If we cannot treat the inciting illness, ICU measures will only prolong death. They may prod our hearts to beat a while longer, but they will never return us home.

As the following chapters will illustrate, *the efficacy of ICU interventions depends upon the reversibility of the underlying illness.* If recovery is possible, then pursuit of aggressive measures may fulfill our God-given call to honor life (Gen. 2:7; Ex. 20:13; 1 Cor. 10:31). When no prospect for improvement exists, however, such interventions prolong death and suffering, and obscure from our vision the glorious truth of Christ's resurrection.

A Hotbed of Suffering

Some have difficulty envisioning how an ICU stay inflicts suffering. To help illustrate the experience, let us imagine a common scenario.

You are rushed to the ICU for difficulty breathing. Doctors and nurses surround you, some of them shouting. They plaster you with monitors, cover your face with a plastic mask, and puncture your arms with needles. All the while, you feel like you're suffocating. The doctors ask to place a tube into your windpipe and put you on a ventilator, but you don't understand their words, and you are too panicked to respond. Suddenly your arm stings—they are injecting an anesthetic, but you don't comprehend this—and you black out.

Later, you awaken to find yourself in an unfamiliar room, with a tube lodged down your throat. The tube makes you cough and gag, and your eyes tear from the irritation. Instinctively you reach for the tube, only to find that your arms are tied to the bed. You scan the room in panic and discover a catheter protruding from your private parts. Frantic, you fight against the restraints. Your nurse gives you a sedative, and then the world goes dark again.

A few hours later, when the sedation lightens, you awaken again, and the horror recurs.

For those of us requiring the most aggressive treatment, these disorienting and frightening ICU experiences can feel nightmarish.

Studies suggest that 60 to 80 percent of people who require a ventilator in the ICU suffer from episodic confusion, hallucinations, and delusions (delirium).[4] In addition, physical pain and discomfort occur commonly. Prolonged bedrest weakens muscles to the point of wasting, and it freezes joints. Pressure upon wasted limbs opens sores in the skin that over time penetrate to bone. Tests involving needles and ultrasound probes occur daily. People with advanced cancer who die in an ICU suffer significantly worse physical and emotional distress compared with those in home hospice.[5] Up to one-third of people who leave the ICU suffer from depression, commonly in reaction to pervasive physical disability.[6] One in five people who survive an ICU stay endure the the unsettling flashbacks and nightmares of post-traumatic stress disorder (PTSD)—the same psychiatric illness that torments soldiers after combat.[7] PTSD afflicts ICU survivors with similar frequency as it did American veterans from the Iraq war.[8]

In addition to the physical, emotional, and psychological toll of intensive care, ICU interventions themselves threaten medical complications. Nationwide efforts focus on reducing the incidence of hospital-acquired infections, 20 percent of which occur in ICUs.[9] Many ICU treatments require catheters and tubes that create portals of entry for bacteria, doubling mortality rate.[10] Breathing tubes, for example, increase the risk of pneumonia. Central lines (chapter 6) required for monitoring and medication administration risk bloodstream infections, and urinary catheters cause—you guessed it—urinary tract infections. Powerful antibiotics used in the ICU can kill bacteria helpful to our gastrointestinal system, paving the way for severe infections with limited treatment options. Paralytic agents, used to relax the chest muscles in severe respiratory failure, place patients at risk for profound weakness that can persist for weeks, prolonging ventilator dependence and ICU stay.[11]

When complications arise from our treatments, they drive us into a state of chronic critical illness. Setbacks counteract small gains in recovery. We limp along in the ICU for months, becoming more debilitated and accruing more injuries as time passes. The outcomes of this cascade are disheartening: 50 percent of people with chronic critical illness die within a year.[12] As we unabashedly strive for recovery, ICU measures themselves can steal our hope for cure.

Far from Heaven

Although God has blessed us with the capability to care for one another in remarkable ways, the man-made trappings of the ICU reside far from heaven. Our interventions are imperfect, as we are imperfect: "There is not a righteous man on earth who does good and never sins" (Eccles. 7:20). When a disease cannot be cured or even improved, aggressive ICU measures embody futility. They inflict suffering without hope of resolution and deprive us of the ability to pray, worship, commune with other believers, and meditate upon Scripture. To chase after futile treatments that deprive us of spiritual nourishment is to strive after the wind and to discount our hope in Christ crucified (Eccles. 1:14; 1 Tim. 4:10; 1 Pet. 1:3).

To address end-of-life issues under such duress requires that we carefully tease apart the benefits and limitations of each intervention and carefully consider likelihood for recovery—all with God's Word fueling our inquiry. In all circumstances, keep these questions in mind:

- Is the life-threatening process reversible?
- What is the best conceivable outcome?
- How much suffering does this treatment inflict?
- How will pursuit of this technology influence my walk with the Holy Spirit?

Most importantly, the edifying clarity of God's Word may guide us. As we strive to discern God's will, the apostle Paul again offers wisdom:

> I appeal to you therefore, brothers, by the mercies of God, to present your bodies as a living sacrifice, holy and acceptable to God, which is your spiritual worship. Do not be conformed to this world, but be transformed by the renewal of your mind, that by testing you may discern what is the will of God, what is good and acceptable and perfect. (Rom. 12:1–2)

A Shared Pain, but Not Punishment

Before we move on, one more topic deserves attention. Families report higher rates of depression, anxiety, and complicated grief when they lose loved ones in the ICU, as opposed to in the home or in hospice.[13] As was the case with the mother who held her daughter in her arms as she died, so deep is our heartache, so immense the pressures of end-of-life care, that we may doubt God's love. We reason that if we suffer calamity, we did something to deserve it.

At a cursory glance, this thinking appears consistent with principles undergirding the fall, Noah and the flood, and the destruction of Sodom and Gomorrah (Gen. 3:14–24; 6:5–7; 19:24–25). In such narratives, punishment for depravity descends swiftly and violently. The book of Proverbs teaches, "The wage of the righteous leads to life, the gain of the wicked to sin" (Prov. 10:16). Yet to use such passages to argue that our suffering is always deserved ignores myriad instances in the Bible when God engages with suffering not to punish but to accomplish tremendous good.

After Joseph's brothers hurl him into a well and sell him into slavery, the Lord raises him up beside Pharoah and saves his people. "You meant evil against me," Joseph says, "but God meant it for good, to bring it about that many people should be kept alive" (Gen. 50:20). Before restoring a man's sight, Christ explains that his blindness occurred not in penalty for sin but so "the works of God might be displayed in him" (John 9:1–3). Christ delays traveling to his dying friend Lazarus, whom he loves, so that in raising him from the dead he might glorify God (John 11). Even in the case of Job, the introductory chapters of his story reveal he is "blameless" in God's sight and that the calamity that befalls him occurs not as punishment, but as part of a divine plan to defeat the adversary (Job 1–2).

Such passages warn that we must never presuppose to know God's intent for someone in anguish. God has infinite capacity to effect goodness in the midst of suffering. No theorems hem in his glory. The cross reveals in luminous brushstrokes our Lord's mercy and grace and his overflowing love for us, made manifest in the death and resurrection of his own Son. In the most magnificent sacrifice the world has known, the Lord allowed suffering, not to punish us but to *save* us. The misery of ICU treatments need not stamp out our joy. Our hope wells forth not from our circumstances but from the Spirit residing in us through Christ crucified.

Take-Home Points

- After initial resuscitation from an acute, life-threatening event, care transfers to the ICU for meticulous monitoring and support.

- Measures implemented in the ICU are *organ supportive*, not curative. They augment or replace the function of failing organs until the process causing critical illness can be reversed.

- If an underlying disease process is reversible, ICU technology can save life. If not, such measures prolong suffering and death.

- Both patients and loved ones report high rates of depression, anxiety, and post-traumatic stress disorder after critical illness.

5

MECHANICAL VENTILATION

When we declare, "I don't want to live on machines," we usually have a ventilator in mind. The very idea of breathing machines evokes nightmares from science fiction movies, with contraptions overriding the natural order of things and, in so doing, destroying our humanity. During the rare occasions when we consider ventilator support,[1] such macabre imagery misleads us toward overly simplistic conclusions. Either we refuse a breathing machine under any circumstances, or in a burst of bravado we insist upon "doing everything."

A Complex Issue

At the bedside, questions of breathing support are far more nuanced. Some cases involve a limited time on the ventilator, with a full recovery afterward. If we reject a ventilator in such circumstances, we risk carelessly discarding the life God has entrusted to us. In other situations, the ventilator controls every aspect of breathing and continues indefinitely without promise of improvement. If we insist upon treatment in the face of futility, we disregard the promise of new life in Christ.

How do we discern our path? The question is not as much one of right and wrong as of recognizing God's grace in either ushering us toward recovery or calling us home to heaven. Our job is to humbly walk the road he forges for us.

To help us visualize the way, we will review the capabilities and limitations of breathing support—when they harm, when they help.

At the Bedside

Each morning I would stumble through medical questions, and she would poke fun at the overstuffed pockets of my medical student coat.[2] To humor me, she would share recipes for her favorite dishes. I would pause in listening to her lungs as she retold stories of family reunions on the beach.

Then, one day, her breathing quickened. She complained of nausea, and her lips paled to the color of nightshade. An alarm sounded as the oxygen level on her monitor dropped. I called for help. Moments later, a crowd of physicians and nurses rushed into the room. I retreated behind them as my supervising resident forced air into her lungs manually with a bag mask.

Her kidneys had failed, and fluid normally removed through the urine had backed up into her lungs. Dialysis would solve the problem, but in the meantime she needed a short period on a ventilator to support her breathing and keep her alive. She had no advance directive, so my team had an urgent conversation with her family.

To our surprise and dismay, her family insisted she would never want to be on a ventilator. Period. Despite the urgings of my team, they remained insistent. They gathered around her to say goodbye, and an hour later, the room fell silent.

The entire ordeal turned my stomach. That morning she had joked with me about my ridiculous pockets. That afternoon she was gone. I remembered our early morning conversations and grappled with the reality that she would never return to the seaside family barbecues she loved so much.

Afterward my chief resident collapsed into a chair in the residents' lounge with consternation darkening his face. He wrung his hands and stared at the floor.

"There's nothing you could have done," a colleague offered.

He shook his head. "This was not okay. She just needed dialysis. We're only talking a day or two on the vent. That's it."

"Her family said she wouldn't have wanted the vent, under any circumstances."

"Not for two days? Really? How well did we explain things to them? Did we really explain that she could be better in two days?"

As the medical student on the team, I listened to their conversation and silently wrangled with my own remorse. I remembered the distress that had washed over her like a tide, the panic widening her once jovial eyes.

I feared we had failed her miserably.

The Basics of Breathing

Breathing (respiratory) difficulties threaten life because they disrupt the crucial exchange of oxygen and carbon dioxide to and from the bloodstream. As discussed previously, every cell in the body requires oxygen to produce energy. Each time we inhale, air fills our lungs, and oxygen enters the bloodstream. When we exhale, carbon dioxide, a by-product of cell metabolism, passes from the blood vessels back out into the air through our lungs. As our cells need oxygen, and as carbon dioxide is dangerous at high concentrations, this gas exchange is essential to life.

Numerous processes hinder breathing, but, in general, we need a breathing machine for three main classes of problems: airway obstruction, excess carbon dioxide, and low oxygen.

1. Airway Obstruction

Your airway is the conduit that carries air to and from the lungs. It consists of your mouth, throat (pharynx), windpipe (trachea), and tubes that branch from your windpipe into your lungs (bronchial tree). Blockage of the airway is life threatening because oxygen can no longer reach your lungs. Conditions that create this emergency include:

- choking
- swelling of the airway from severe allergic reaction
- blockage of the airway from tumors, blood, or pus
- unconsciousness, for two reasons: (1) soft tissues in the back of the throat block the airway, and (2) inability to cough up saliva, vomit, or mucus

When airway obstruction is imminent, clinicians place a silicone tube (endotracheal tube) into the windpipe to keep it open and connect the tube to a ventilator.

2. *Excess Carbon Dioxide*

Carbon dioxide makes the blood acidic, which in turn disables proteins that are vital for life. To thwart this process, our body triggers us to breathe faster and more deeply when carbon dioxide levels climb. If disease impairs removal of carbon dioxide through the lungs (a process called ventilation), carbon dioxide can rise to lethal levels. Examples of conditions that inhibit carbon dioxide clearance include:

- chronic obstructive pulmonary disease (COPD, also known as emphysema)
- sedative or pain medication overdose (e.g., from narcotics)
- thyroid disorders
- stroke
- brain injury
- widespread infection (sepsis)
- spinal cord injury
- disorders leading to muscle weakness, e.g., myasthenia gravis
- abdominal swelling that hinders movement of the diaphragm

Supplying extra oxygen is not enough to treat problems with carbon dioxide. Such emergencies call for the support of breathing *mechanics*—the physical maneuvers of inhalation and exhalation—with a ventilator or BiPAP machine (see below).

3. Low Oxygen

A low oxygen level (hypoxia) is the most common indication for a ventilator. Causes of low oxygen levels are numerous and include:

- fluid within the lung tissue (pulmonary edema)
- fluid within the chest cavity (pleural effusion)
- infection of the lungs (pneumonia)
- obstruction of the small airways with mucus
- lung scarring (fibrosis)
- bleeding of the lungs
- clot within the blood vessels of the lungs

Supplemental oxygen from a tank can treat mild hypoxia, but severe cases require the extra air pressure attainable only with a ventilator or BiPAP machine.

This long list of conditions hints at the innumerable possible outcomes with ventilator support. In airway obstruction, the lungs often work normally, and you may be weaned from the ventilator as soon as the airway issue resolves. If you have excess fluid in your lungs, you may need only a few days of BiPAP support and no tube in your windpipe. On the opposite end of the spectrum, if you have severe emphysema and chronic weakness of your breathing muscles and develop a drug-resistant pneumonia, a ventilator may quickly transform from a temporary measure into a permanent fixture. When considering measures for breathing support, thorough discussions with a doctor who knows you well are crucial. Vague assumptions and sweeping generalizations will only lead you astray.

An Overview of Mechanical Ventilation

Mechanical ventilators, while a gift, remind us how technology falters in comparison with God's perfect design. When we draw a breath, our diaphragm lowers, our rib cage expands, and the resultant negative pressure gradient siphons air into our lungs. The motion is smooth, unlabored, and elegant. In contrast, a ventilator helps you breathe by *pushing* air into your lungs. A breath on the ventilator is a maneuver of force. We can finely adjust targets in pressure and volume for each breath; however, the mechanism, and often the subjective experience, is unnatural.

In the most benign of circumstances, a ventilator supports your own efforts to breathe. You trigger each breath yourself, according to your own natural rhythm, and the machine gives you an extra push. After delivering a set volume or pressure of air, the ventilator clicks off, and you exhale naturally. On such settings, the ventilator inflicts less discomfort. People who are struggling for air often report significant relief after going on the ventilator.

On the other hand, mechanical ventilation for severe respiratory failure tightly controls lung mechanics with a precision so unnatural that you require sedation and paralysis to endure it. You may need to be positioned face-down in the hospital bed, which leads to significant facial swelling and skin sores. The recovery from such an ordeal lasts months, with prolonged ventilator dependence a distinct possibility.

I first witnessed the distressing effects of mechanical ventilation not as a doctor but as a teenage daughter, when my father underwent an emergency operation. When he awoke from the surgery that saved his life, my mother and I sighed with relief. We had no idea that he, in contrast, was terrified. Still confused from his anesthesia, he gagged on the tube lodged in his windpipe, sensed the ventilator overriding his attempts to breathe, and panicked. While my mother held his hand and softly reassured him, he tugged against the restraints and signaled in desperation that something was terribly wrong. "I felt like I was suffocating," he later explained. "I thought I was having a heart attack."

Decades later, I have watched my own patients endure the same unsettling experience. Some, especially the most severely ill, recall little from their time on the ventilator, remembering only the discomfort of endotracheal tube removal. However, up to two-thirds of ICU patients recall details of intubation and ventilation.[3] Afterward they describe pain, fear, loneliness, lack of control, anxiety, and lack of sleep.[4] Inability to speak especially challenges people, with 50 percent of ventilated patients describing moderate to severe stress as they fight to communicate.[5] These communication difficulties during ventilation are linked with anxiety and depression long after recovery.[6] Furthermore, as with so many of our interventions in critical care, the ventilator itself can inflict injury. Delivery of excessively high volumes of oxygen and pressure can damage lung tissue, and in some cases this injury can collapse the lung. Additionally, up to 5 to 15 percent of ventilated patients develop pneumonia, which confers a mortality rate of 10 percent.[7] Given these risks for suffering, those with severe baseline impairment or terminal illness should carefully deliberate with a trusted doctor about whether a ventilator will help or offer only anguish.

Endotracheal Intubation

Ventilators and endotracheal intubation go together; one always accompanies the other. With intubation, a clinician guides a silicone tube directly into your airway to ensure a stable connection between the ventilator and your lungs. As you can imagine if you have ever experienced water going "down the wrong pipe," an endotracheal tube is highly irritating. The natural response to anything lodged in the throat is to cough and gag. Given this impulse to cough the tube out, most require sedating medications to prevent tube dislodgement. Furthermore, when you awaken from sedation, your first instinct is to reach for the tube, so wrist restraints are standard safety precautions in the ICU. This combination of disturbances—the sensation of a foreign body in your airway, followed by the realization that your arms are tied down—frequently incites panic. People on the ventilator often plead for tube removal, and those who have experienced intubation in the past loathe the idea of undergoing it again.

In addition to inflicting significant discomfort, intubation increases risk for pneumonia. Within as little as a few hours after intubation, a film of bacteria lines the inner wall of the tube, creating a reservoir that can infect the lungs.[8] The risk of pneumonia increases with every day spent on the ventilator and is a major source of mortality in the ICU.

Tracheostomy

After seven days of intubation, pressure from the endotracheal tube ulcerates the vocal cords and can scar the windpipe.[9] To avoid these complications, doctors often recommend tracheostomy (trach, pronounced "trake") for anyone on a ventilator for more than two weeks. In this procedure, a tube is surgically inserted through the neck and into the windpipe, just below the Adam's apple. The endotracheal tube is then removed from the mouth, and the trach is connected to the ventilator.

At first glance, the idea of surgical connection to a breathing machine seems subversive, even ghoulish. However, life with a trach can trouble us less than we might presume. When struggling through critical illness, the ability to communicate your thoughts, concerns, and fears can offer solace. Tracheostomy facilitates this interaction, even while you still require the ventilator. Removal of the endotracheal tube from the mouth eliminates the need for sedation and allows you to mouth words, write, or use letter boards to communicate with clinicians and loved ones. Eventually, a tracheostomy permits you to transition off the ventilator and undergo speaking trials, with a plan to remove the trach altogether when you no longer require breathing support.

The most important question to consider with tracheostomy is whether, in your unique circumstances, the procedure implies long-term ventilator dependence. If a trach is another step toward recovery, we may embrace the risks. On the other hand, if it signals a prolonged death while ventilator dependent, we should question its worth.

Noninvasive Positive Pressure Ventilation

In some reversible cases of breathing failure, a less-invasive option of lung support called noninvasive positive pressure ventilation (NIPPV) can help. Also called CPAP or BiPAP depending on its settings, NIPPV is essentially a ventilator connected to a face mask. I will use the most familiar term, BiPAP, for the rest of this discussion.

While you're on BiPAP, clinicians strap a tight-fitting mask to your face, and the machine provides extra air pressure with each breath you take. As you require no tube in your windpipe, you remain awake and communicative, and the mask may be removed and replaced at intervals with little consequence. BiPAP is most effective for quickly reversible problems, e.g., fluid in the lungs or a severe asthma attack. Over the last decade, BiPAP has also entered the homes of people suffering from sleep apnea.

Although less obtrusive than a ventilator requiring a tube, BiPAP does confer risks. If you have claustrophobia, you may tolerate the tight-fitting mask poorly. BiPAP requires you to initiate your own breaths, which may not be feasible in severe illness. The constant flow of air into the mouth risks stomach distension and vomiting as well as impaction of oral secretions within your lungs. These latter points render BiPAP a bad option if you are drowsy and confused,[10] as without the ability to cough you can easily develop pneumonia. More ominously, in cases of acute respiratory distress syndrome (ARDS), a condition in which widespread illness triggers lung damage, BiPAP actually worsens survival.[11] Furthermore, if a trial of BiPAP fails, the risk of death is actually higher than if a ventilator with a tube was used from the start.[12] Those of us with rapidly reversible causes of respiratory failure stand to benefit most from BiPAP; those of us with more insidious breathing difficulties may suffer further harm from it.

Transient Support versus Prolonged Ventilator Dependence

When we cite our wishes against a breathing machine, we are often thinking about *long-term* ventilator dependence. We may not consider the instances when a brief period of support promises to return us home. For example, everyone who undergoes general anesthesia for a surgical procedure requires a brief period on a ventilator. Even a simple operation for appendicitis or for a diseased gallbladder requires a short time of ventilator support. Few of us object in these circumstances, because we anticipate that after completion of the operation the tube will be removed, and we can go home.

Remorse still gnaws at my heart when I think of my patient from medical school days who died from fluid in her lungs. Would she really have refused a ventilator if she had known that her breathing difficulties would resolve in two days? When a breathing machine promises to restore us to a full recovery, many of us will accept its temporary discomforts. And as God's image bearers, we often should.

On the other hand, for those of us with crippling baseline lung disease or those walking in the twilight of life, the arduous experience of mechanical ventilation may worsen our suffering needlessly. Weaning from the ventilator increases in difficulty as days in the ICU accumulate. The more support a machine provides, the less work our muscles perform to breathe. With disuse, these muscles degenerate, and eventually we lack the strength to breathe independently. The longer we remain on a ventilator, the greater the challenge to free ourselves from it.

Yet even here, we must be careful not to overgeneralize. We may develop ventilator dependence but suffer little if we still engage with loved ones and partake in activities we find meaningful. For example, people with profound weakness from neurological diseases may require a ventilator long-term but can still enjoy life-giving fellowship. To ascertain for ourselves, and for our loved ones who cannot speak, the best course of action regarding ventilator support, we must pay close attention to the clinical outlook at hand, the duration of ventilation in question, and most importantly our unique attributes that render such treatments as paths either to desolation or to hope.

As we tackle the issue, the scriptural principles introduced in chapter 2 must guide our hearts and minds. Given our unique story, does a ventilator promise preservation of God-given life or prolonged suffering and death? How does it influence our ability to serve God and to live out the fruit of the Spirit (Gal. 5:22–23)? How can you provide Christian witness as your own breath fails?

The following additional questions may guide you as you contemplate your situation. Ideally, such deliberations should occur in depth, with a doctor, tailored to your individual narrative, and *before* life-threatening illness robs you of speech.

- How will the diseases I manage daily influence my ability to wean from a mechanical ventilator?
- In cases of mechanical ventilation among loved ones, how reversible is the condition driving respiratory failure?
- For how long can we anticipate a need for the ventilator?
- What is the likelihood for long-term ventilator dependence?

Trust in the Lord

When faced with the tragic challenges of modern medicine, we take refuge in the God who knows us: "O LORD, you have searched me and known me! You know when I sit down and when I rise up; you discern my thoughts from afar" (Ps. 139:1–2). We revel in the gift of his Word, which itself is "breathed out by God" (2 Tim. 3:16). While our days in this world vanish on the wind—"Surely all mankind stands as a mere breath" (Ps. 39:5)—his breath unseats mountains and weaves galaxies (Pss. 18:15; 33:6). Even if we gasp for air, he is with us. We rest in the assurance that he loves us and that he sent his Son to die for us so that we might know him. Whether we breathe with the aid of a machine or relinquish our breath at life's end, we have the hope of the risen Christ. Remember that when all is finished, we will breathe anew (1 Thess. 4:13–18).

Take-Home Points

- Mechanical ventilators support breathing in the setting of respiratory failure.

- The ramifications of ventilators vary. In reversible conditions, ventilator support is often transient and minimal. In severe illness, ventilators assume complete control of lung mechanics, require sedation to tolerate, and can progress to long-term ventilator dependence.

- Ventilators incite emotional turmoil from fear, loss of control, and an inability to communicate, as well as discomfort from the breathing tube.

- Whether a ventilator offers promise of life or prolongation of death depends upon the likelihood of weaning from it. Baseline health conditions, reversibility of respiratory failure, and degree of ventilator support influence the outlook for recovery.

6

CARDIOVASCULAR SUPPORT

Vasopressors, Inotropes, and Lines

Medications that support blood pressure and heart function (called vasopressors and inotropes, respectively) garner little controversy compared with CPR and ventilators, but they can still create a conundrum for the loved ones of the dying. These powerful drips are ubiquitous in the ICU, and in many circumstances they serve as a barometer for the severity of an illness. Families at the bedside quickly learn that a decreased dose of medication written on a nurse's hourly flowsheet means "better" (as less support is needed), and they cling to this tangible reflection of a loved one's progress.

Unfortunately, critical illness is much more complicated than this simplistic correlation implies. While in clinical practice, I regretted the frequency with which loved ones, heartened by an improving vasopressor requirement, struggled to comprehend a family member's imminent death. From the vantage point of the ICU doorway, it can be difficult to discern that a declining dose does not always signal recovery. In this chapter I hope to illustrate the uses and limitations of these medications so that in critical situations, we can better understand how they function. Throughout, let us draw our peace from the assurance that Christ has overcome death. "For this light momentary affliction is preparing for us an eternal weight of glory beyond all comparison" (2 Cor. 4:17).

At the Bedside

For three months, his family took shifts and rearranged schedules so he would never suffer alone. They relinquished wages and graduations so that throughout the long days and nights, while nurses wiped sweat from his brow and drew blood, love would linger with him.

His life before the hospital had been rich yet fragile. He filled his days with card games, grandkids, and pondside strolls, but he engaged in these from his wheelchair, with his portable oxygen tank his constant companion. As the days in the ICU mounted, those moments of cards and water seemed increasingly remote. The days meandered like an ancient winding staircase. Sometimes they inclined, wound, or crumbled, but overall they proceeded downward.

He was never weaned from the ventilator. After three months the machine still creaked and sighed through his tracheostomy like a bellows. A continuous dialysis machine hummed in the corner of his room. He spent most of these days clouded in delirium, although he would occasionally scowl. Every so often, in a fleeting burst of lucidity, he would shove his nurse away during an attempt to clean him or to dress his bedsores. Their eyes would lock, and the nurse would try to steel herself beneath his fierce gaze as he mouthed, "No!"

His family exchanged worried glances whenever he protested ongoing care. Yet when the nurses gently inquired about changing his care goals, dread blanched their faces. Through a sheen of tears, they would scan the room for an escape.

They found a foothold in the array of bags, pumps, and tubing that dripped medications into his veins. "How much blood pressure medicine does he need today?" they would ask. "The same as yesterday. The vasopressor dose hasn't changed," the nurse would answer. "Well, that's good news!" they would exclaim. "That means he's stable!" Their enthusiasm mismatched their haggard expressions.

The morning he died, his bloodwork revealed shutdown of nearly every organ system. He had already lost function of his lungs and kidneys. Under the stress of yet another infection, his liver also failed, and his blood could no longer clot. He sank into irrevocable multiorgan failure.

We met with his family to guide them through the end. After we laid out all the harrowing details, they held one another and wiped tears from their eyes. Yet they remained unconvinced.

"I don't understand," one of his sons said. "You're telling me everything is worse, but his vasopressors are the same dose as yesterday. They haven't gotten worse. It doesn't seem like he's dying, based on that. I think we should keep going."

"The vasopressor dose is just one piece of the puzzle," I tried to explain. "His lab results show us that his organs are failing. Soon, his blood pressure will follow."

"Well, I think we should wait until that point. I say we keep going until God makes it abundantly clear to us."

"He's in a lot of pain," his nurse interjected with concern. "He's dying. We shouldn't prolong it."

"I don't agree that he's dying," his son shot back. "I mean, you're always writing these numbers down, every hour. Now you're telling me they don't matter?"

We agreed to continue treatment but not to escalate any doses of his medications. In a few hours, the patient's blood pressure drifted downward. As the numbers slunk into ominous territory, his family agreed to transition to comfort-focused care. They crowded around him, as they had for so many months. They alternated between holding his hands and stroking his forehead as they said goodbye.

The Basics of Blood Pressure

Most of us in the US worry when our blood pressure is too high. We cut salt from our diet, exercise, and take medication so that when we sit upon the examination table and the blood pressure cuff squeezes our arm, our doctor smiles and repeats a "good number": 120/80, 110/70, or maybe even 100/60. Such lifestyle changes to lower blood pressure protect against heart disease, kidney failure, and stroke.

In the ICU, severe illness creates the opposite problem. When blood pressure falls too low, our blood can no longer deliver oxygen throughout the body. Cells soon die, followed by the organs they constitute, and fatal multiorgan failure ensues.

Blood pressure plummets when at least one of the following mechanisms fails:

1. the pump action of the heart
2. the volume of blood in our blood vessels
3. the ability of blood vessels to constrict and dilate

In bleeding and dehydration, for example, blood pressure drops as the volume of blood in our vessels decreases. In heart failure, the heart cannot contract with sufficient strength to produce adequate blood pressure. In severe allergic reaction (anaphylaxis) or widespread infection (sepsis), blood vessels inappropriately dilate and cannot maintain the resistance necessary for normal blood pressure. The umbrella term for all these conditions is *shock*, i.e., inadequate blood supply to the organs. In all cases of shock, restoration of blood pressure to the organs is essential to survival.

Vasopressors and Inotropes

Infusions of blood or fluid into our veins can treat shock from bleeding or dehydration but at other times inotropes and vasopressors are necessary to maintain blood flow to organs. Infusions of these medications run continuously, and nurses carefully adjust the doses to meet specific targets.

Inotropes enhance the ability of the heart to pump and are useful in cases of heart failure. Vasopressors (or pressors), on the other hand, constrict blood vessels that have inappropriately dilated. Every blood vessel in the body contains a layer of muscle, and under normal circumstances, this muscle tightens and relaxes—much like your bicep—to regulate blood pressure. When blood vessels dilate inappropriately, the blood pressure falls to dangerous levels. Conditions that trigger this phenomenon include infection and allergic reaction, spinal cord injury, brain injury, and medications that sedate or treat pain. In such instances, pressors constrict blood vessels to restore normal pressure. Examples of popular vasopressors and inotropes are listed in the glossary.

Most pressors and inotropes are so powerful that they require the use of specialized catheters for safe administration and monitoring. We will next review these catheters, so common to ICU care.

Central and Arterial Lines

Inotropes and pressors are given through specialized catheters that allow medical staff to infuse these powerful drugs safely and to monitor their effects moment to moment. The two most commonly used catheters in the ICU are arterial lines and central lines. Most of us admitted to the ICU with severe illness will require one, if not both, of these lines, and during long ICU stays we may need them replaced several times.

Arterial catheters, often called "A-lines," measure blood pressure continuously. They are usually placed in the wrist, but sometimes they will be inserted into an artery in the elbow crease, underarm, or groin. They instantly detect changes in blood pressure and are more reliable than the traditional blood pressure cuff used in doctors' offices. They also permit frequent blood draws without repeated needle sticks, and when connected to specialized devices they provide information about the function of the patient's heart.

Central venous catheters, commonly called "central lines," are threaded into a large vein close to the heart. They administer powerful medications more safely and effectively than an IV in your hand. Central lines are usually inserted into the neck, below the clavicle, or in the groin.

Complications and Drawbacks

Vasopressors, inotropes, central lines, and A-lines are the mainstay of support for patients in shock. However, as with all ICU interventions, their usefulness has limits, and they confer risks.

While rare, blood vessel injury during A-line placement can require surgery.[1] Clot within or surrounding the catheter can threaten blood flow to the hand or foot, also requiring urgent intervention.[2]

Central lines require local anesthetic to place, and the sterile drapes necessary to place the catheter cleanly may induce claustrophobia. More concerning, up to one-third of cases of central lines induce complications, including bloodstream infection, bleeding, vessel injury, and lung collapse.[3]

Inotropes also carry risks. In certain situations you can suffer a heart attack while on an inotrope. Furthermore, these medications can pitch the heart into dangerous, life-threatening rhythms.

Vasopressors have risks too. When we endure profound shock, constriction of our small arteries with pressors can actually damage our organs, *even when measured blood pressure is normal.*[4] The high doses of pressors necessary to increase blood flow to the heart and brain can paradoxically restrict blood to our limbs, such that our hands and feet blacken, die, and require amputation. This process can also occur in the intestines, leading to bowel perforation that requires emergency surgery, as well as in the liver and kidneys, causing their failure.

The gentleman at the beginning of this chapter developed this very kind of progressive organ failure. Although pressors maintained pressure within his large arteries, the blood flow to his organs was insufficient. His blood pressure appeared normal, which is why his loved ones strained to understand his decline.

Near the end of life, shock often becomes refractory; in other words, increasing doses of pressors yield no response. In refractory shock, doctors may increase doses of pressors to astronomical levels, with little change in blood pressure. At this stage, further interventions to stave off death are futile.

Fearfully and Wonderfully Made

For those of us lingering at the bedside of a loved one in the throes of critical illness, the simplicity of numbers can offer a tempting anchor. Doses of medication go up, and things look worse. They decline, and hope takes flight within us.

Although *in general*, doses of pressors and inotropes correlate with illness severity, this is not always the case. Just as God sculpts us into unique, complex, mysterious, elegant beings in his image, so also he knits us together with an ornateness that our paltry technology can support but never duplicate. We are "fearfully and wonderfully made," the workings of our blood vessels, hormones, cells, synapses, mind, passions, memories, and gifts "intricately woven" (see Ps. 139:13–16). ICU technology allows us a window into these exquisite workings, but just as we cannot distill our own complexity to a single word or trait, so also must we assess all facets of illness when we consider the nearness of heaven. Medications are just one piece of the puzzle, and especially when they have potential to hurt, to cling to them and ignore other details skirts toward idolatry.

Above all, whether numbers unsettle us or embolden us, our hope resides not in the dosages meted out by pumps but rather in Christ. Only in him may we find peace and rest (Matt. 11:28).

Take-Home Points

- Vasopressors and inotropes are powerful medications that support blood pressure and heart function.

- Administration of these medications requires insertion of arterial and central venous lines. These catheters are ubiquitous in ICU care but confer risks of infection, clotting, and vessel injury.

- In the ICU we can measure blood pressure within large arteries but cannot discern or control blood flow through the small vessels that supply organs. As a result, although we can adjust vasopressors to achieve a normal blood pressure, the extremities, intestines, kidneys, and liver may suffer permanent damage.

- Inotropes also have limits, with high doses conferring risks of heart attack and fatal arrhythmia.

- We may be tempted to use pressor and inotrope doses as a way to measure progress. However, these numbers represent single data points. Just as God made us in his image as complex and intricate beings, a solitary number cannot exclusively predict life or death.

7

ARTIFICIALLY
ADMINISTERED
NUTRITION

Few end-of-life issues rival artificially administered nutrition in public controversy. The tragic case of Terri Schiavo captured media attention in the early 2000s, as debates about whether to remove her feeding tube after fifteen years in a vegetative state went up the echelons of the judicial system, all the way to the Supreme Court.[1] Tragic images of loved ones kissing her elicited emotional and polarizing responses from human rights advocates, the president of the United States, and even the Vatican.

While all end-of-life dilemmas incite conflict, our conscience recoils at the notion of withholding nutrition. When we cradle an infant and satisfy her cry for milk, our provision of food flows with tenderness. The equivalence of food with compassion persists into adulthood, manifested in holiday feasts, quiet everyday meals with family, and dinners over which we fall in love. Memories that shape us abound with overflowing tables.

In contrast, artificially administered nutrition bears little resemblance to these meals and traditions that sustain us. Artificial food arrives at the hospital as a beige liquid packaged in plastic bottles. Tubes and pumps replace candlelight and place settings. From the doorway, artificially administered nutrition seems more akin to a medical intervention than to the human experience we all covet, and yet the thought of withholding such nourishment strikes us as subversive, even inhumane.

In many cases, withholding tube feeds *does* fly in the face of our biblical call to love one another (Matt. 22:39; John 13:34–35). A well-meaning and frightened son under my care once refused a temporary feeding tube for his mother, who had suffered a stroke, out of conviction that she would never want to be dependent on tubes and machines. Yet in her case, the tube was a temporary measure necessary for her recovery. After a lengthy and painful debate involving the ethics committee, she received the feeding tube and two months later had it removed when she could eat again.

Conversely, the tube is often ill-advised for a dying patient. The intestines shut down at the end of life. Force feeding as death nears creates painful cramping and bloating, and the tubes themselves are uncomfortable and fraught with complications. As our lives draw to a close, we may elect to simply feed ourselves as able, without artificial sources of nutrition. The Bible does not require us to lengthen our dying, and our view of the cross should coax us to loosen our grip on futile interventions.

At the Bedside

Every morning I would find her propped in a chair, facing a window to gaze at the sunrise as it spilled onto the Charles River. Sometimes she wouldn't notice me as I entered; her mind was so intent on the flecks of gold dancing upon the water. Yet even as the early morning bathed her in its glow, she would cough, and her breathing would rattle.

"How are you doing?" I asked one morning.

She shrugged. She was trapped in a hospital at the end of life. Once she left the ICU, she would transition to hospice. Whether it was her sorrow or her own fragile breathing that stole her words, she spoke little.

I motioned to my own nose. "No more tube?" I asked.

She grimaced and shook her head. "No more," she said.

"She took it out overnight," her nurse, who had appeared behind us, interjected. "The team didn't think it was right to push her about replacing it."

I turned to the patient. "Food and drink might make you cough and make your breathing worse."

"I know," the patient answered. "I get it. But I can't take it. I just want a popsicle. Or ice cream. Tube . . ." she gasped for breath, "tube is awful."

"I'll get you a popsicle," I promised. She smiled wearily before returning her attention to the cascade of light upon the river.

When I returned with a popsicle and a container of ice cream, I found her son in the room, standing above her and glowering.

"You can't eat, Mom," he insisted. "It will make your breathing worse. You *need* the feeding tube." He glimpsed the packages in my hands and scowled at me. "Doctor, what are you doing?"

"She asked me for a popsicle and some ice cream."

"Are you serious?"

"She is."

"No way. If she's hungry, she needs the tube back in her nose. Her pulmonologist said if she eats, she could get pneumonia again." I could see tears brimming in his mother's eyes as she watched us. Worried our exchange would further upset her, I ushered her son out of her room.

"I can't begin to imagine how upsetting this is for you," I said in a hushed voice. "But she's about to go on hospice. We need to focus on her comfort right now."

"But how can she live on popsicles and ice cream? She's going to starve to death. The cancer taking her is one thing, but I don't think it's right to starve her. She needs the tube."

"She's taken the tube out herself three times now and doesn't want it replaced. It's not a good solution for her."

"Then what about placing one surgically?"

"That carries a greater risk of hurting her than the ice cream does."

He chewed the side of his lip and stared at the ground as he shook his head. "I don't know about this. I don't like it. I need to talk to our priest; see what he thinks."

When we returned to the room, she no longer explored the glimmering horizon. With her eyes cast downward, she wept softly and stared at the blank linoleum floor.

When Might We Need Artificially Administered Nutrition?

Numerous medical problems impair our ability to feed ourselves. Critical illness diminishes appetite, as anyone sick with the flu can attest. Feeding by mouth in the setting of mechanical ventilation, sedation, brain injury, and delirium either risks choking or is frankly impossible. Diseases of the gut, e.g., pancreatitis, bowel obstruction, poor blood flow to the intestine, diverticulitis, and intestinal bleeding often prohibit a normal diet. Furthermore, the procedures and tests so frequent among critically ill patients can interrupt nutrition delivery.

Aside from its weighty ethical significance, nutrition is essential for recovery.[2] The stress of critical illness provokes our enfeebled bodies to break down muscle for energy, consuming their own mass.[3] Additionally, poor nutrition weakens our bodies' immune system, exposing us to dangerous infections. These effects lengthen our ICU stay, prolong our time on the ventilator, and speed death.[4]

To protect against these hazards, ICU doctors provide calories through a tube entering the gut or through a catheter in the veins. In the following pages, we will review these different types of nutrition to discern when they can help and when they might inflict undue suffering. Throughout, let us remember that our hope springs not from tubes but from the gospel.

Tube Feeds and Nasogastric (NG) Tubes

The simplest method of tube feed delivery, and often the first employed in the ICU, is a nasogastric (NG) tube. This plastic tube passes through the nose, down the throat, and into the stomach. Usually an NG tube is stiff and about a quarter of an inch in diameter, comparable to the dimensions of a large drinking straw. The wide caliber of the tube allows clinicians to remove stomach contents in the event of nausea by connecting the tube to a suction cannister on the wall. When risk of vomiting is low, a weighted, smaller, and more flexible tube can be more comfortable. In the setting of mechanical ventilation, physicians may insert the tube through the mouth, alongside the endotracheal tube, instead of through the nose.

The discomfort of an NG tube requires little explanation. Imagine a pencil up your nose, as well as a perpetual sore throat that worsens each time you talk or swallow. Unsurprisingly, those of us with delirium instinctively remove NG tubes, forcing nurses to restrain our arms to the bed. Nasogastric tubes can also irritate the nasal passages, leading to nosebleeds and sinusitis. Their placement carries a rare, but very serious, risk of malpositioning within the airways instead of the gastrointestinal tract, leading to life-threatening lung collapse (pneumothorax) or pneumonia.[5] Finally, as a nasogastric tube keeps open the ring of muscle between the stomach and the esophagus, these tubes lead to regurgitation and inhalation of tube feeds in 25 to 40 percent of cases.[6]

Nurses connect a feeding tube to a pump that administers formula in preprogrammed volumes, usually continuously at a rate of one-third to one-half cup per hour. Tube feeds may trigger diarrhea, especially among the elderly and when medications are administered through the tubes.[7] Physicians and hospital nutritionists add fiber to limit diarrhea, but patients may require a small tube placed in the rectum to control spillage and to prevent skin irritation and ulceration from loose stool.

Gastrostomy Tubes (G-Tubes)

If we require nutrition support for longer than four to six weeks, doctors may recommend surgical placement of a gastrostomy tube. Commonly referred to as a "G-tube" or "PEG" (for percutaneous endoscopic gastrostomy), this tube passes through the abdominal wall directly into the stomach. G-tubes provide more effective and consistent nutrition delivery than NG tubes, and there are fewer episodes of tube clogging.[8] When implemented wisely, a G-tube provides nutrition critical to recovery when we cannot feed ourselves. Those of us afflicted with brain injury, debilitating stroke, advanced Parkinson's disease, or long term swallowing disorders, to name only a few diagnoses, may especially benefit from G-tube placement.

G-tube placement requires the skills of a surgeon, gastroenterologist, or interventional radiologist. The procedure itself carries risk of injury to the colon, small intestine, and liver, which occurs infrequently but can cause infection or bleeding that necessitates further surgery.[9] Dislodgement of the tube within the first week of placement can also leak gastric acid and food into the abdominal cavity, triggering life-threatening infection and earning us a second trip to the operating room. Infection of the abdominal wall around the G-tube occurs in up to 30 percent of cases, requiring antibiotics at minimum and abscess drainage or widespread cutting away of infected tissue in the worst scenarios.[10]

Major complications occur infrequently with feeding tubes, but when they do, the ramifications can be catastrophic. I once cared for a teenage girl who survived multiple injuries from a car crash, only to die from leakage of stomach contents into her abdomen after her G-tube dislodged soon after placement. Another elderly and frail woman held on through major cardiac surgery but died from pneumonia when her feeding tube was inadvertently threaded into her lung.

In the hospital, no intervention is without risk. The key question, as we consider ICU care in the shadow of the cross, is whether the likely outcome justifies the risks.

Total Parenteral Nutrition (TPN)

Total parenteral nutrition, or TPN, provides nutrients and calories when our gastrointestinal tract is unusable. The high concentrations of salts and proteins in TPN can clot small veins, so TPN requires a central line. This indwelling line, as well as effects of TPN on the immune system, increases the incidence of infection and lengthens the ICU stay for patients receiving TPN.[11] Studies suggest that these risks have decreased in recent years and may continue to do so as methods improve; however, current guidelines track away from this particular method except in cases where other options aren't feasible.[12]

Does Feeding Help or Hurt?

As heavily as decisions about ventilators and resuscitation weigh upon us, ethics seem even murkier with artificially administered nutrition. Our Christian obligation to care for one another includes attention to hunger and thirst: "Then the King will say to those on his right, 'Come, you who are blessed by my Father, inherit the kingdom prepared for you from the foundation of the world. For I was hungry and you gave me food, I was thirsty and you gave me drink" (Matt. 25:34–35). Feeding the hungry is a moral imperative as we minister to the vulnerable:

> If a brother or sister is poorly clothed and lacking in daily food, and one of you says to them, "Go in peace, be warmed and filled," without giving them the things needed for the body,

what good is that?" So also faith by itself, if it does not have works, is dead. (James 2:15–17)

As Christ loved us, so must we feed the hungry among us.

Yet what if artificially administered nutrition, with its battery of pumps and tubing, worsens suffering or shortens life? How many times shall we replace a nasogastric tube when our husband with dementia, upset and panicked, wrenches it from his nose? At the end of life, as our bodies wither and the workings of our intestines grind to a stop, must we cram our stomachs with formulas that cause bloating, cramping, and diarrhea?

Although it cannot assuage heartache at the bedside, medical knowledge can offer guidance in a few scenarios. As the vignette at the beginning of this chapter suggests, artificially administered nutrition rarely helps at the end of life.[13] Although we cringe at the thought of depriving loved ones of nourishment, tube feeds cause bloating, abdominal pain, nausea, vomiting, and diarrhea that actually *worsen* discomfort during our final days.[14] Additionally, as the cardiovascular system and kidneys fail, the extra volume from tube feeds backs up into our lungs, causing coughing, shortness of breath, and a sensation of drowning.[15] During our final days, when cure is no longer attainable, forced feeding through tubes hardly represents loving care.

We may worry about suffering from hunger and thirst at the end of life. Yet without functioning intestines, hunger occurs rarely, and feeding with tubes may only prolong our dying without providing any comfort. Simply wetting the mouth, which is a standard practice in palliative care, significantly abates thirst. If a loved one wishes for small amounts of food or liquid at the end of life so that she may enjoy taste and avoid thirst, *we should provide these* by mouth, with care and affection. What greater love can we show one another than to offer food and drink by hand? If unconsciousness precludes such hand feeding, we need not worry about suffering from hunger and thirst and should not risk nausea and vomiting with compulsory feeding.

End-stage dementia is another condition in which artificially administered nutrition threatens harm. Alzheimer's and other diseases of cognitive decline complicate swallowing, generate apathy toward eating, and create dependence upon others for feeding. Although tube feeding may seem attractive in such scenarios, data suggest the contrary. In fact, research shows that G-tubes incur such significant harm and offer such scant benefit that both the American and Canadian geriatrics societies recommend against artificially administered nutrition in advanced dementia.[16] Feeding by G-tube does not improve survival, augment nutritional status, avoid aspiration, or reduce the incidence of bed sores.[17] People stricken with dementia frequently pull at and dislodge feeding tubes, necessitating emergency room visits and the use of restraints, which only further distress those already struggling with confusion.[18] To nourish and care for loved ones suffering from dementia, the most compassionate approach is hand feeding for as long as possible, a tactic that encourages life-giving intimacy and social interaction in addition to providing nutrition.

In contrast with cases of dementia and dying, the role of artificially administered nutrition among those with severe neurological injury, as in the case of Terri Schiavo, is more complicated and controversial. Coma and persistent vegetative state (see chapter 9) render people unconscious and unaware of pain. Artificially administered nutrition in such cases should not cause physical discomfort, although it might invite complications through recurrent inhalation of the food, or diarrhea, or tube dislodgement. Tube feeding in severe brain injury may also prolong our lives under conditions that conflict with our convictions about life and service to God. Decisions in these cases are highly individualistic and depend on our personal concept of suffering and our understanding of life in Christ. We will discuss concerns about brain injury and advance directives in greater depth in chapters 9 and 12. For now, I recommend that as you consider this issue, you examine the facets of life that have enabled you to serve God in faith and love and consider how severe brain injury and tube feeding would transform your walk with the Spirit.

The Bread of Life

While we navigate difficult choices with our own faculties and free will, ultimately our lives depend upon God's grace: "Man shall not live by bread alone, but by every word that comes from the mouth of God" (Matt. 4:4). God provided food from heaven for his people in the wilderness (Ex. 16:11–12). Jesus fed five thousand people with a child's portion of bread and fish (Matt. 14:13–21). "I am the bread of life," he said. "Whoever comes to me shall not hunger, and whoever believes in me shall never thirst" (John 6:35). While such verses may not direct our decisions about feeding tubes and formulas, they offer comfort. While we should seek to feed the hungry in love, we need not force calories into our failing bodies in the twilight of life. Through Christ, we cling to a nourishment far richer than any tube can provide.

Take-Home Points

- When critical illness impairs our ability to eat, physicians can provide nourishment artificially.

- Nutrition can be delivered through tubes entering our gastrointestinal tract through the nose or abdominal wall or via catheters placed in large veins. Of these two modalities, tube feedings, in general, are preferred for their lower infection risk.

- Artificially administered nutrition creates uncomfortable side effects, including diarrhea, bloating, discomfort from tubes, and infection.

- Although we may be tempted to pursue nutrition at all costs, we must realize that its drawbacks may be burdensome in specific scenarios. In particular, at the end of life and in advanced dementia, tube feeding worsens discomfort without proven benefit.

8

DIALYSIS

Organ failure warns of life-threatening illness at minimum and impending death at worst. Some of the sickest people in the hospital require a ventilator for respiratory failure. Heart failure claims the lives of hundreds of thousands each year. Liver failure deranges nearly every system in the body, progressing until transplantation is the only life-saving option.

Until the 1940s, renal failure followed this pattern and was always fatal. The advent of dialysis, however, has transformed renal failure from a death sentence into a chronic medical problem. In contrast with other classes of organ failure, we can supplement or replace kidney function for as long as decades. The unusual case of dialysis poses its own unique dilemmas as we consider end-of-life care, so in this chapter we will review those peculiarities and tease out when it can preserve life and when it threatens to prolong suffering and death.

At the Bedside

For three weeks, she drifted in and out of delirium. She would cry out to loved ones long departed as nurses dressed sores on her buttocks. At one end of her bed, a continuous dialysis machine alternately murmured or blared its alarms to announce a clotted circuit. At the other, a tree of IV pumps issued pressors into her bloodstream. Throughout it all, her husband, stooped with age, sat beside her and intermittently held her hand.

She had severe disease of her heart valves but was too ill to undergo cardiac surgery. Her failing heart could no longer tolerate the routine hemodialysis that had supplemented her shriveled kidneys for decades. Even on the gentle continuous dialysis in the ICU, her blood pressure dipped to dangerous numbers, and she required increasing doses of pressors to keep her alive.

Her dialysis access—the conduit between her bloodstream and the machine—posed recurrent problems. The surgically constructed fistulas in her arms had clotted years ago and now lurked useless beneath skin riddled with bruises and scars. After veins in her neck also clotted, she relied upon a stiff catheter in her groin; with that catheter in place, she could no longer bend her legs or get out of bed.

For weeks, heart and kidney specialists grappled over options for her. She could not withstand procedures to reconstruct her heart. With her heart valves narrowed and leaking, her blood pressure dropped precipitously low with every attempt at dialysis. Were she ever to leave the hospital, her heart would not withstand dialysis at an outpatient center.

After each somber conversation with her husband, he would listen to our words, then look at his beloved. "I hear what you're saying, Doc," he would finally answer in a low, subdued drawl. "But she's my wife. Just do what you can, please. You gotta help her."

One morning, her dialysis catheter failed again. She would need yet another procedure to replace the line in order to resume dialysis. The nurse practitioner who cared for her delivered the news with slumped shoulders. "Should we really replace this catheter?" she asked. "I mean, what's our end point? How much more can we do to this poor woman?"

As if on cue, the senior kidney specialist (nephrologist) crossed the ICU to speak to us. "We have no more options," he admitted. Although eighteen patients occupied the ICU, we knew about whom he spoke.

"We've feared the same for a while," I said.

"I know. I just had a long conversation with her husband. He's having a hard time, but at this point further dialysis is futile. Please, don't replace her catheter. I'll discontinue the dialysis orders."

Her nurse, who had listened warily to our conversation, breathed a sigh of relief. "He's going to be heartbroken," she said with a tremulous voice. "But it just needs to stop. All she does is moan in pain and shout for people who aren't here. What we're doing to her is awful."

Back in her room, we found her husband with his head in his hands.

"You're giving up on her," he groaned when we entered. "You can't stop the dialysis. She'll die if you do."

I placed a hand on his shoulder and felt the bones beneath his shirt shudder against my palm.

"I'm sorry. I know it's so hard. But we can't get her well. Nothing we're doing is helping her, and if we continue, we'll only be hurting her."

"I've been with this woman for sixty years," he answered, his jaw set. "I promised God I'd cherish her always. But now you're telling me that I'm losing her. That I've failed her. How can I accept that?"

An Introduction to Kidney Failure

Shifts in the volume of urine you excrete daily hint at the versatility of the kidneys and their capacity to tightly regulate the fluid in your body. Your kidneys filter toxins and maintain the normal balance of water, electrolytes, and acid in your bloodstream. They moderate blood pressure and influence platelets that help form blood clots when you injure yourself.

In kidney (renal) failure, excess fluid leaks out of the bloodstream, soaking your lungs and swelling your limbs. Potassium and sodium, both vital for the function of your heart and nerves, rise to dangerous levels. The acid concentration in the blood increases, further worsening breathing and disrupting the delicate balance your cells require to function. By-products of metabolism, normally removed through the urine, linger in the bloodstream and can cause confusion, which if left untreated progresses to delirium and even stupor. If end-stage renal failure is left untreated, drowsiness progresses to coma, and you can develop fatal respiratory failure or a dangerous heart rhythm. Until the advent of dialysis, this was the outcome for most with kidney failure.

Supporting the Kidneys When They Fail

A host of long-standing conditions can cause chronic kidney impairment, among them diabetes, chronic heart failure, liver cirrhosis, and autoimmune diseases. Kidney failure in these scenarios often occurs gradually over months to years until it declines to a point requiring dialysis.

In contrast, kidney failure in the ICU usually occurs suddenly, often secondary to shock. As discussed in chapters 3 and 6, dehydration, bleeding, widespread infection, and acute heart failure are common culprits. Kidney failure in this setting is a common problem, affecting 35 to 67 percent of ICU patients, but the majority recover, with only about 5 percent of people requiring dialysis.[1] Those who need dialysis, even in a temporary fashion, are often the most severely ill, with over 50 percent dying in the hospital.[2]

When shock occurs in those of us who are otherwise vigorous, kidney injury is often reversible, with only a brief decline in function. The kidneys still produce urine, and physicians simply monitor the kidneys.

More severe damage, when urine production stops entirely, may prompt ICU physicians to give diuretics, i.e., medications that stimulate the kidneys to filter fluid and remove potassium. If these medications cannot control the dangerous effects of kidney failure, and laboratory values and symptoms threaten life, nephrologists start dialysis.[3] Sometimes dialysis is only a temporary measure; however, in the most extreme cases, when shock is profound or when chronic medical conditions predispose us to kidney damage, kidney failure can be permanent. In such cases we continue dialysis after we leave the ICU and over time receive care from a nephrologist who determines whether we will need a kidney transplant.

Understanding Dialysis

Dialysis mimics the kidneys by restoring the normal chemical environment of the bloodstream. Specifically, it filters out dangerous accumulations of electrolytes and waste products and replaces these with safe amounts of molecules key to life. Dialysis also eliminates excess fluid that would otherwise saturate the lungs.

Ninety-four percent of people with end-stage kidney disease in the US receive hemodialysis, usually at specialized outpatient centers.[4] In hemodialysis, blood is pumped into a specialized machine where it is filtered and then returned to you through a catheter or surgically altered blood vessel. You will usually require hemodialysis three times weekly, with each session lasting three to five hours. Long-term hemodialysis requires a surgically created connection between an artery and a vein in your arm designed to withstand the high pressures of dialysis. In an urgent setting, a catheter, similar to the central lines described in chapter 6, can fulfill this requirement; however, chronic use of such lines risks infection and increases mortality.[5]

In the ICU you are usually too sick to tolerate the rapid fluid shifts necessary for hemodialysis to work. To achieve dialysis safely in the ICU, clinicians use continuous dialysis, which is essentially hemodialysis that runs continuously at a gentle, slow rate. Continuous dialysis still filters the blood but does so slowly to avoid the swings in blood pressure so hazardous for ICU patients. Once you stabilize from shock, physicians may try taking you off continuous dialysis and transition you to hemodialysis.

In many cases of severe and sudden kidney injury, we cannot know the likelihood for kidney recovery for weeks, sometimes even months. Such predictions involve review of multiple data points over time, with careful consideration of your baseline medical conditions. When considering if dialysis will be temporary or long-term, ongoing and explicit conversations with your kidney specialist are crucial.

Living with Dialysis

Although dialysis can sustain us for years, it so alters daily life that sufferers compare its burdens to those of cancer and HIV.[6] A three-times weekly hemodialysis schedule jeopardizes independence and our ability to work, constraints that can dishearten us as we seek to serve the Lord through our vocation. An array of distressing physical symptoms also accompany dialysis. More than half of patients who require chronic hemodialysis report crippling fatigue, bone pain, sleep disturbances, and pain from repeated needle sticks at the dialysis access site.[7] Unsurprisingly, depression arises frequently among those who suffer such symptoms.[8]

In the US, patients who require dialysis are quite sick in general, with an annual mortality rate of 20 percent, and as high as 60 percent within a year of initiating dialysis.[9] This high death rate among dialysis recipients exceeds that in other countries, possibly due to the greater burden of advanced cardiovascular disease in the US.[10] The take-home point from such statistics is that the need for dialysis should trigger conversations about the burden of disease. Dialysis should prompt questions about our overall risk for prolonged suffering with aggressive treatments.

When Dilemmas Arise

Decisions about whether to start or continue dialysis can distress us. In the scenario described at the beginning of this chapter, the fragile patient suffering from irreparable heart failure had no further options for recovery. In her case, continuing dialysis would delay death for a short time but at the cost of prolonged suffering without reprieve. Without avenues for cure, dialysis represented a futile intervention.

To her doting husband, however, dialysis had been her lifeline for decades. During all those long years, during the wearying litany of complications, setbacks, and bad news, he had remained at her side. From his point of view, to stop dialysis meant abandoning his life partner when she needed him most.

Issues surrounding dialysis are so highly complex that in recent years, specialists have proposed guidelines to discern when dialysis threatens to harm.[11] These guidelines recommend against dialysis when our prognosis from other illnesses is poor, e.g., if we have advanced cancer or end-stage cardiovascular disease.[12] Similarly, dialysis can be harmful if we require restraints or sedation to tolerate it, e.g., if we suffer from advanced dementia and are prone to pulling out dialysis needles.[13]

Dialysis guidelines attempt to improve communication about end-of-life issues. Although over 20 percent of people on dialysis die annually, in one study from 2013 only *30 percent* discussed life-sustaining measures with their nephrologist.[14] This statistic is disturbing in light of high mortality rates among elderly patients who start dialysis. In one study, among nursing home residents older than seventy years of age, within one year of starting dialysis 58 percent had passed away, and 87 percent suffered a progressive decline in vigor and independence.[15] Although chronic kidney failure increases our risk of death and debility, few of us who need dialysis discuss end-of-life care.

Should We Withhold or Withdraw?

In the outpatient setting, we have ample time to discuss whether dialysis aligns with our goals of care. In contrast, when kidney failure occurs suddenly, threat to life eliminates the luxury of time. Urgency compels us to make decisions about dialysis quickly, with scant opportunity to carefully weigh the options.

Conflicts about dialysis in the ICU fall into two general categories: (1) whether to withhold dialysis in a patient with sudden, new-onset kidney injury, or (2) whether to stop chronic dialysis when other illness threatens life. In the remaining sections of this chapter we will explore some questions to better organize our thoughts when dealing with such dilemmas. As always, the priorities of protecting God-given life, acknowledging God's authority, and extending mercy must steel us.

Questions to Ask

While statistics can reduce highly complicated issues to concrete checkpoints, they cannot capture the stories, fashioned by experience and our God-given dignity, that transform an issue from perfunctory to heart-wrenching. Especially in the case of dialysis, an organ-supporting technology that can sustain us for years, our unique tapestry of life experiences, personality traits, values, and medical history should guide us. As we decipher whether dialysis would honor God through protection of life belonging to him, or whether it would constitute cruelty, we must keep the preciousness of each person as an image bearer—and our hope in the gospel—at the forefront of our minds.

A few questions can help us navigate the waters. I would encourage discussing these points at length with a trusted physician.

Is the illness responsible for kidney failure reversible?
As we have discussed in preceding chapters, the effectiveness of any life-supporting technology depends upon the reversibility of

the causative illness. If kidney failure occurs secondarily to a recoverable infection, dialysis may preserve life. In contrast, if it arises from progressive disease without potential for improvement, as in the case of the woman with untreatable heart failure at the start of this chapter, then dialysis may prolong death and inflict suffering without benefit.

How do other medical conditions influence likelihood for survival?

A condition that is manageable in an otherwise healthy patient may devastate those of us shouldering serious illnesses. For example, a young man without previous health problems who develops pneumonia has a greater chance for recovery than does one already crippled with advanced diabetes, chronic heart failure, and end-stage emphysema. Guidelines suggest that dialysis harms more than helps those of us older than seventy-five years who at baseline have extensive comorbidities, severe malnutrition, and limited independence.[16] In such cases, we should pursue dialysis only with caution.

What is the best foreseeable outcome if I accept or continue dialysis?

Any treatment we accept should help us to leave the hospital, to engage in activities we find meaningful, and to interact with those we love. When dialysis extends life without promise for recovery and discharge from the hospital, we risk prolonging the process of dying.

If my kidney failure is new, what is the likelihood that my kidneys will ever recover? Will dialysis be temporary or permanent?

The probability of being weaned from dialysis after recovery from a life-threatening illness depends on individual medical problems and the cause of kidney injury. In some circumstances, e.g., among patients with severe cardiovascular disease, physicians can easily predict long-term dialysis dependence. Often, however, clinicians cannot make an assessment until the acute illness improves. If doubt exists, and if no progressive terminal illness threatens life, it is reasonable to pursue dialysis for a short term, until time clarifies prognosis.

If dialysis will continue long-term, how will it cause suffering? How will it benefit me?

The answers to these questions differ for each of us. Those of us still blessed with vigorous health may find the inconvenience of hemodialysis a small price to pay for continued time engaged with family in the pursuits dear to us. Those who already struggle with incapacitation, however, may find the rigors of dialysis unbearably burdensome.

* * *

When these questions point us toward withdrawal or refusal of dialysis, we must surround one another with prayer and support. The timing of death from acute kidney failure varies, but, on average, within one week toxins accumulate within the bloodstream to steep us in coma. In the most severely ill among us, the time course may be shorter. Our mandate to love one another, as Christ loved us (John 13:34–35), is never more critical than in these moments.

Whatever our struggle, however we strive, let it be for the glory of God. Remember the cross. Remember that whatever our circumstances, Christ has overcome death. "As each has received a gift, use it to serve one another, as good stewards of God's varied grace: whoever speaks, as one who speaks oracles of God; whoever serves, as one who serves by the strength that God supplies—in order that in everything God may be glorified through Jesus Christ. To him belong glory and dominion forever and ever. Amen" (1 Pet. 4:10–11).

Take-Home Points

- Our kidneys filter wastes from the bloodstream and maintain a normal balance of electrolytes and acid.

- Kidney injury occurs commonly in the ICU, and the majority of patients recover. A small percentage of the most severely ill, however, may require dialysis either temporarily or long-term.

- Dialysis replaces kidney function, most commonly by filtering blood through a machine.

- Chronic dialysis use allows patients to survive with kidney failure for years but does impose burdensome physical effects, as well as detriments to lifestyle and independence.

- Patients who require dialysis are often quite sick at baseline and have a high mortality rate.

- Discussions about whether to pursue dialysis should focus on the needs of each individual, with careful attention to other medical conditions and the degree of suffering that dialysis inflicts.

9

BRAIN INJURY

The brain serves as the control center for the rest of the body.[1] Our patterns of awakening and falling asleep originate within the brainstem. Hormones that control our metabolism, our temperature, and the characteristics that make us male and female arise from the brain. So do our memories and dreams, our fears, our decisions, and our abilities to compute arithmetic and contemplate Shakespeare. Our brain sends command signals to our muscles whenever we lift a child into our arms. When we admire the sunrise, nerves carry the information from our eyes to a visual processing center in the brain, and a network then effects changes in separate areas to elicit wonder and to compare the palette of colors with other inklings of beauty.

The functions of the brain are so highly complex and interconnected that we have limited capacity to support the brain and virtually no technology to replace it. Dialysis can substitute for failed kidneys. A ventilator delivers oxygen to compromised lungs. Yet no intensive-care technology can reproduce the intricacies of a memory or restore emotions. Brain injury dismays caregivers because its effects can devastate patients, and yet we have a meager arsenal against it.

At the Bedside

He was barely a teenager. As I examined the gunshot wound in his head, I struggled to focus on my duty rather than the horror of it all. Paramedics found him unresponsive, not breathing. An endotracheal tube jammed into his windpipe elicited no response—not even a cough or a gag, let alone wakefulness. When I flashed a penlight into his eyes, his pupils remained dilated and fixed, impervious to all glimmers of life.

A battery of tests confirmed brain death. When we met with his mother, the patient's blood pressure had already precipitously declined. His heart rhythm adopted an erratic pattern on the monitor.

After tears, she leaned toward him and searched his face. Years of laughter, trials, and memories illuminated her eyes. "God blessed me with the most wonderful child," she said. "And now he's called him home."

Months later, another teenager arrived at the ICU with severe head trauma. His exam and tests also pointed to brain death. Another boy we could not save. Another heartbreaking conversation.

I sat with the patient's father, and my colleagues and I delivered the grim news in measured beats. Afterward, I leaned toward him to narrow the expanse between us. He sat motionless, his arms folded across his chest, his gaze like stone.

"No," he said after a pregnant moment. "He's going to live." He pointed an index finger skyward. "From Jeremiah: 'Nothing is too difficult for God. With God all things are possible."

Framing the Problem

These two cases capture the anguish and misunderstanding that surround brain injury. Clinically, both patients mirrored each other. Both were teenage boys. Both had devastating head trauma leading to brain death. In both cases, their parents responded with grief, and with faith. Their loved ones' remarks, however, reflect opposite ends of a spectrum. In the first case, the patient's mother voiced her acceptance of God's authority and of the inevitability of death. In the second, a grieving father clung to his conviction that the Lord would cure his son, regardless of a doctor's counsel that the injuries were fatal.

Although we cannot know the stories, grief, and spiritual journey that informed each parent's response, their reactions reflect the confusion that besets families of brain-injured patients. Numerous factors contribute. News outlets use the terms *coma* and *brain death* interchangeably, despite marked differences between these conditions. Tragic, controversial cases, such as that of Jahi McMath, further vex the public and heighten distrust of doctors.

Perhaps most unsettling, from the doorway, patients with brain death may appear identical to those with reversible injury. Both types of patients may require a ventilator to support their breathing. In brain death the heart still beats for a while, and initially the skin appears flushed and feels warm. Brain dead patients may even *move*. These reflexive movements—arising from the spinal cord, not the brain—can deeply perplex and distress loved ones and stir up distrust of a physician's assessment.

Differentiating between brain injury states requires neurological examinations and adjunct tests, information few loved ones feel equipped to decipher in the midst of devastating news. Understanding begins with clarifying the terminology wielded with such haphazardness in popular media.

An Introduction to Brain Injury

Brain injury occurs in stages. In primary brain injury, an initial insult—e.g., a trauma, a stroke, a ruptured aneurysm, or a prolonged lack of oxygen (as with cardiac arrest or near drowning)—damages brain tissue. Brain tissue swells in response to injury, as all tissues do. (Consider how a finger warms and reddens when cut or broken.) The skull is a rigid, closed space that cannot expand, so when brain tissue swells, the pressure within the skull increases. In severe brain injury, this rising pressure impedes blood flow to and from normal brain cells. As a result, after severe trauma or a stroke, initially spared areas of the brain can suffer secondary damage from lack of oxygen-rich blood.

Medical and surgical efforts to support us after brain injury focus on limiting this secondary brain damage. In the most extreme circumstances, surgeons remove a portion of the skull to relieve pressure. In other cases, they guide a monitor into a space within or surrounding the brain to measure pressure. Such measurements guide ICU physicians in the administration of medications to reduce swelling. Doctors also sedate us, tightly regulate our breathing, artificially increase our blood pressure, and cool us to a normal temperature all to reduce swelling, improve blood flow, and give uninjured areas of the brain the best chance to survive.

Untangling Definitions

In focal brain injury, we suffer impairments in specific areas, e.g., in movement of one side of the body or in the ability to speak. Depending upon the degree of disability, as well as such factors as age and pre-injury health, we may improve with aggressive physical, occupational, and speech therapy. Neurologists can offer guidance regarding the anticipated extent of recovery.

In contrast, the most devastating brain injuries—those popular media most often misrepresent—impair consciousness. When damage affects either the entire cerebral cortex or areas of the brainstem responsible for arousal, *coma* results. In coma, you are unconscious and unaware of your surroundings. You may breathe independently, but you do not respond to any stimulation.

Slightly less damage may produce a *vegetative state*, in which you have sleep-wake cycles and open your eyes but do not respond to the environment. The term *vegetative* understandably upsets families, who may associate it with *vegetable*. The phrase actually derives from Aristotle's three forms of life, with *vegetative* indicative of the capacities for nutrition and reproduction but not thought. If you are in a vegetative state, you are wakeful but unaware of the people and events around you.

In coma and vegetative state, you often improve only minimally; however, upon first diagnosis you still have *potential* for some recovery. Your restored function may range from dramatic to minimal to nothing at all. You may depend upon nursing and medical care for the rest of your life. With regions of the brain intact, however, some improvement is *possible*.

Brain *death* constitutes a different category. In whole brain death, injury is so catastrophic that *all* brain tissue dies. As the control center for the body, when the brain dies, the other organ systems soon follow. Unlike coma and vegetative state, tissue injury is total and irreversible, without potential for recovery.

Coma and Persistent Vegetative State

In some cases of severe brain injury, imaging studies (i.e., CT scans and MRIs), combined with bedside neurological exams and a review of risk factors (advanced age, poor stamina, nontraumatic type of injury), warn of a poor chance for recovery quite early. In such circumstances, we must partner with physicians to determine the best course of action, and lean into Christ, the perfecter of our faith (Heb. 12:1–3).

In other cases, doctors cannot predict improvement immediately. In fact, guidelines recommend against labeling a patient's vegetative state as "persistent" (i.e., expected to be permanent) earlier than three months after an inciting stroke or cardiac arrest.[2] Cases of head trauma require even more time, with uncertainty persisting for up to a year.[3] Practitioners must also be vigilant to rule out locked-in syndrome, a condition in which you are awake and aware, but appear to be in a vegetative state due to widespread paralysis.

Although miraculous stories populate the media, most commonly "improvement" in severe head injury means progressing from coma to a persistent vegetative state, or from a vegetative state to consciousness with severe disability. As you are unconscious, if you are in a coma or vegetative state you experience no pain or discomfort; interventions to extend life until the prognosis is clear will not inflict unnecessary suffering. However, the longer we require twenty-four-hour care for our basic needs, the more complications we accrue: pneumonia, wound infections, bed sores, tube dislodgements, and life-threatening blood clots. In cases without hope for recovery, aggressive measures such as tracheostomy, long-term mechanical ventilation, and artificially administered nutrition may prolong dying rather than preserve life.

If, as we consider our own lives, we cannot envision serving the Lord under such circumstances, we need not accept or pursue feeding tubes and ventilators for chronic, severe brain injury. However, our aim in forgoing such interventions should never be to *speed* death (Ex. 20:13). Food and water should still be offered to us by mouth, if possible. Care should never cease, although as we will review in the next chapter, its focus may shift from cure to comfort. While forgoing a feeding tube may hasten death, our intent must be avoidance of burdensome treatment, not quickening demise. Compassion and mercy—and fear of the Lord—must drive us (Hos. 6:6). When we care for brain-injured loved ones amid our own shock and despair, we must focus on the commandment to love one another (Mark 12:30; John 13:34) and consider how a loved one would direct his own care if he still had a voice.

The Difficulty of Brain Death

Brain death, or "death by neurologic criteria," occurs when the *entire* brain dies from lack of blood flow. Prior to advances in intensive care, brain death and cardiopulmonary death—i.e., cessation of breathing and heartbeat—happened concurrently.[4] When the brainstem died, breathing stopped, oxygen levels plummeted, and cardiac arrest occurred. In modern ICUs, however, ventilators interrupt this process. Brain dead people have no functioning brain cells, but if a ventilator artificially provides oxygen, intrinsic cardiac pacemakers separate from the brain drive the heart to beat for a time.

In the majority of cases, this time of continued heartbeat remains brief. Most brain-dead people develop cardiovascular collapse within hours to days, in spite of aggressive ICU interventions.[5] In the majority of cases, when our brain dies, the rest of the body quickly follows.

In 1980, the Uniform Determination of Death Act (UDDA) legally recognized death by neurologic criteria in the United States.[6] According to United States law, we die either when our heart and lungs stop working or when our entire brain dies. The rationale follows that as the brain is the "control center" of the body, when the brain dies, life cannot persist.

Both medical and Christian establishments have affirmed the stipulations of the UDDA. The American Academy of Neurology has published guidelines on brain death determination since 1995.[7] In its ethics position statement, the Christian Medical and Dental Association likewise recognizes "irreversible cessation of all clinical functions of the entire brain" as death.[8] Even the Catholic Church has officially legitimized death by neurological criteria.[9]

However, for a parent at the bedside of his beloved teenager whose cheeks still sport the ruddy blush of youth, these claims can seem impossible to embrace. Even after death of the brain, spinal cord reflexes can trigger movements such as turning the head, flexing the fingers, and raising the arms. Such movements offer no hope for recovery, yet they can mimic a response to a mother's voice or squeezing a brother's hand. We may not grasp that a loved one will never breathe again, or perceive, or think, but we understand a hand squeeze. Such reflexive movements elicit from us a visceral response, raw with love and desperation.

How can Scripture guide us during such devastating circumstances? How can we focus our prayer, when doctors utter words we dread to hear?

Sanctity of Life

The Bible teaches that life is God's sacred gift to us: "He himself gives to all mankind life and breath and everything" (Acts 17:25). As our Creator, he formed us from the dust and fashioned us in his own image (Gen. 1:26; 2:7; Ps. 139:13). He charges us to protect the life he has created (Gen. 2:15; Ex. 20:13).

A brain death determination often requires us to trust the assessment of a physician whom we have never met. Given the stakes, we should feel empowered to *ask questions*. Despite nationwide legal recognition of brain death, the United States has no national, evidence-based standards of brain death determination. Diagnostic practices vary across regions and institutions.[10] University hospitals in the United States usually adopt an institutional protocol for brain death declaration, and physicians should review the details of the protocol with families upon request. At minimum, a diagnosis of brain death requires that no other condition contributes to a patient's poor neurological exam. Patients must have a normal temperature and blood pressure, without evidence of intoxication, poisoning, severe infection, or electrolyte imbalances. Further tests at the bedside, including a test for the drive to breathe, establish the absence of cerebral and brainstem function. Any doubt of the diagnosis after such tests can be explored through additional studies to evaluate blood flow within the brain.

With our loved ones' lives in balance, we have every right to *ask explicit questions* about how the medical team has reached a determination of brain death and to *seek counsel* from a member of the clergy whom we trust. We are God's handiwork (Eph. 2:10). As those who cherish God's workmanship, we are entitled to understand the death of our beloved in detail.

In Death, New Life

Death, even brain death, does not mark the end. In the wake of the cross, we find an everlasting hope. Even while we mourn, and while we wrestle with anguish, we rest assured that Christ has *already* overcome and has swallowed up death in victory (1 Cor. 15:54–55). Those who fall asleep in Christ will join Christ in resurrection (1 Thess. 4:13–14). Paul writes that "neither death nor life, nor angels nor rulers, nor things present nor things to come, nor powers . . . will be able to separate us from the love of God in Christ Jesus our Lord" (Rom. 8:38–39). And that truth sustains us, beyond the horror, beyond the tears, into the arms of our Savior.

The promise of God's grace may sustain us even when we're unsure if a loved one is a believer. Whatever our loved one professed during consciousness, only the Lord knows the heart. And we serve a God of abundant goodness. When we anguish over the fate of a loved one, we can lean into Abraham's profession: "Shall not the Judge of all the earth do what is just?" (Gen. 18:25)

If hope for meaningful recovery from brain injury persists, we should feel empowered to prayerfully pursue it. If, however, brain death occurs, or if brain injury permanently deprives our loved ones of their capacity for worship and faithful service, we need not chase after wind. We may rest in the promise of Christ's resurrection and in the new life that awaits us when God calls us home.

Take-Home Points

- Brain injury occurs along a continuum, with mild impairment on one end of the spectrum and whole-brain death on the other. The popular media, unfortunately, uses terms like *coma*, *vegetative state*, and *brain death* interchangeably, although they are very different clinical entities.

- Coma and vegetative state refer to severe brain injuries that impair consciousness but have the *potential* for improvement. Prognosis in such conditions often takes months, with the likelihood for recovery dependent upon the type and extent of brain injury.

- In brain death, the entire brain dies. This injury is irreversible, with no hope for recovery. Cardiac arrest usually quickly follows a diagnosis of brain death.

- Pursuit of aggressive interventions in severe brain injury is an individual decision. Loved ones can rest assured that unconscious patients experience no pain, so interventions undertaken until prognosis is clear will not inflict suffering. On the other hand, we should not feel obligated to accept burdensome treatments without potential for recovery.

- In the United States brain death is legally equivalent to death. However, controversies persist on clinical and ethical fronts. We should feel empowered to ask questions when a diagnosis of brain death is issued and to discuss the issue at length with trusted doctors and pastors.

PART 3

DISCERNMENT at LIFE'S END

10

COMFORT MEASURES
and HOSPICE

In this chapter we tread toward the somber moment when treatments only hurt. Until now, we have examined the intricacies of organ-supporting technology in detail to clarify when they might promise to restore our God-given lives, or when they threaten to incur further suffering and rob us of moments spent in prayer and with those we love. Now we step over the threshold to the moment when death confronts us. This transition can pitch loved ones into a tumult of confusion, guilt, and heartbreak, with long-lasting repercussions.

At the Bedside

During our discussions he reminded me of a puff of dandelion seeds, the translucent wisps barely intact, the entire assembly ready to disappear with one overzealous breath. He seemed wholly unprepared for the burden he carried.

My colleague, a senior critical-care trainee, leaned toward him across the table. "Did you have a chance to think about everything we talked about yesterday?" he asked.

He raked his mustache with his bottom teeth. "Yes."

"Okay. Good. I'm glad you had a chance to think things over. What are your thoughts?"

His bottom lip quavered. As the tears filled his eyes, he searched both of us. "She's my mom," he implored. "She's all I got."

"I know this must be so hard."

He studied the floor, and nervously tapped his foot against the carpet.

"It's so hard to make decisions like this, for someone you love. But your mom is dying. We can't cure her."

"I know. But I can't do what you're asking me to do."

"I know it's so hard, but— "

"You don't know the half of it," he shot back. "You doctors know a lot of stuff, and you're just doing your job. I get that. But she's my mom. I can't pull the plug on my mom."

"We would never 'pull the plug,'" my colleague said. "We're asking you to please allow us to focus on treating her pain and discomfort now and stop things that won't help."

"I get everything you're saying. But I can't do it. She's my mom. She never gave up on me."

I studied his face, the eyes still wet and desperate, the ends of his mustache now damp with tears. His bottom lip still quivered. The delicate scaffolding that held his composure trembled, ready to give way.

"Can you please tell us about her?" I asked. He looked at me, guarded. "We don't know her the way you do," I added. "What is she like? What matters to her?"

"She's wonderful," he said, his voice cracking. "She's the most caring person. I know everyone says that about their mom, but she's something special. She still makes me breakfast every morning, just like when I was a kid. She'd do that for me and my brothers after my dad died, and she had to get up at five o'clock in the morning to work. Every morning, the sun wasn't up yet, but she made us a hot breakfast. And she still does it. She always puts us first."

The momentary brightening of his expression faded. "I can't let her go."

"It's clear you love her so much."

He buried his head in his hands. "I can't live without her," he whispered as more tears came. The fluorescent lights beneath which we sat hummed, lending a sharpness and vulgarity to the room unbefitting the tenderness that poured from him. I tried to steady my breath until the tide of his grief swelled to its zenith, then inched back.

"I know she's dying," he finally said. "But what will I do without her?"

"If she could speak to us right now," I ventured softly, "what would she say? What would she tell us mattered most to her?"

He thought for a long moment, then gathered himself, as if mustering what little frayed strength remained within him. "She'd say taking care of us mattered most," he answered. "She'd want to make us that damn toast in the morning."

"And if she knew the situation now?"

Another pause passed. Whether he peered back into unseen memories or ahead onto the grim road forward, he grimaced. He never answered my question.

"Okay," he said with sudden resolve. "So, let's say we stop everything. What if she's scared? What if she doesn't understand, and she gets mad at me?"

"We'll make sure she's comfortable throughout. We'll be certain of that."

"What does that mean, 'comfortable?' You doctors say stuff like I should know what it means, but I don't."

"It means we'll minimize her pain and anxiety as best as we can."

"I don't think I can live with her being scared or feeling alone. I can't let her think I'm giving up on her."

"Of course not. We have medications that can help. And you can stay with her the entire time, if you wish."

"But isn't this killing her?"

"No. Her failing heart, kidneys, and lungs are taking her from us."

He eyed us skeptically. "It feels an awful lot like killing. It feels like I'm giving up on her."

Later, the respiratory therapist turned down the ventilator settings. A nurse disconnected the dialysis, darkened the cardiac monitor, and changed the medications in the infusion pumps. He sat beside her, clutching her hand in his own.

"Can't the tube come out?" he asked.

"I wish it could, but her lungs are too sick. We don't want her to fight for air." He eyed the tube as if it were a serpent in the grass, a sinister thing. A nurse tucked a fleece blanket around her chin, a flimsy token of domesticity meant to soften the sterility of the hospital room, yet the blanket did little to hide the tube protruding like an appendage from her mouth.

We drew the curtain and closed the door to give them privacy. Over the next hour, through the door we could hear him speaking to her. As the peaks of her heart tracing slowed, widened, and eventually flattened into nothing, his words gave way to prayer, and then only to tears, the last gentle and raw outpourings his broken heart could manage.

Changing Focus

The news "We have no more options" can shock us and evoke anger and distrust toward physicians. What is obvious to a clinician seldom is to family members, for whom the array of infusion pumps and the wheeze of the ventilator changes little from one moment to the next. As with this grieving son, we agonize over the right path, our loved one's wishes, and our own grief as we cling to the person we love so dearly.

The traditionally and often carelessly wielded phrase "withdrawal of life support" conveys an unnerving sense of abandonment and offers little consolation as we face a loved one's death.

The crass and inaccurate phrase "pull the plug" further leadens our hearts with guilt. We may fear that when we admit to the imminence of dying, we give up on life and on those we love. While we may understand the futility of organ support, when the time comes to stop aggressive interventions for ourselves, our beloved spouse, or for the mother who tied our shoes as a child, "we just can't."

The emotional and spiritual turmoil these moments inflict persists long after ventilator machines and pumps have switched off. As death nears, the more heavily medicalized the scene, the more patients and families suffer. Research shows that a year after a loved one dies in the ICU, up to 40 percent of family members still grapple with psychiatric illness, including generalized anxiety, depression, post-traumatic stress disorder, and complicated grief.[1] The questions that trouble us strike to the core of who we are as image bearers of God and who we strive to be in Christ. The burdens we shoulder in these days may sap our already depleted strength.

As we navigate these turbulent waters, we must seek courage to *ask questions*, to speak extensively with trusted physicians and clergy, and to take our time as we consider the subtleties of each situation. Critically, we must lean upon the Lord and pray for his mercy and guidance, that his will would be done (Luke 22:42).

Hospice Care

In an ideal scenario, we learn of a life-threatening condition while still in command of our thinking and stamina and discuss limitations of organ-supporting treatment ahead of time with our family and primary doctor. As our condition declines, our mind remains sharp, and we outline our own care: treatments we find acceptable, interventions we do not, and what matters to us most as we serve the Lord in our final days on earth. We seek richness and meaning in our days, even as our bodies wither and break down.

In such circumstances, hospice support can provide us time in the places and with the people we love. In hospice care, an interdisciplinary team, usually comprised of physicians, nurses, social workers, chaplains, and health aides, provides medical care with a focus on symptom control and quality of life rather than cure. Staff partner with us to determine the activities and values most dear to us and help us to achieve our goals in the waning days.

Although medical centers and specialized facilities offer hospice services, hospice care may also allow a significant number of us to spend our final weeks and months at home. In one study of forty thousand cancer patients, 75 percent of those not in hospice died in hospitals or nursing homes, compared with only 14 percent of hospice patients.[2] For those of us who do not imminently require organ-supporting technology, hospice care may offer solace, comfort, and a peaceful environment, in contrast with the sharp edges and mechanized atmosphere of the ICU.

People considering hospice often voice concerns that a focus on symptoms rather than cure will speed death. Ironically, research suggests that oftentimes hospice *improves* survival. People with lung cancer, pancreatic cancer, and congestive heart failure who elect hospice survive significantly longer compared with those who pursue aggressive treatment, with a prolongation of life of up to one hundred days in the case of heart failure.[3] This point merits emphasis: in the final stages of chronic illness, *stopping aggressive treatment can prolong life.* Worded alternatively, at the end of life, if we insist upon dubious treatments, we can actually shorten the God-given life we're fighting to steward. When our last days near, choosing to spend them intentionally, rather than in an institution connected to a ventilator, may not only enhance our moments but also increase their number.

Hospice can also enrich our last days. One study of cancer patients demonstrated no difference in survival among those who elected hospice compared with aggressive end-of-life care, but *did* reveal that hospice patients reported significantly higher quality of life before death.[4] Furthermore, hospice services cut the incidence of post-traumatic stress disorder and complicated grief among caregivers by 75 to 80 percent.[5] With its focus on time well spent, hospice can help us focus on prayer and on the relationships with which God has blessed us. It provides opportunities for preparation and closure, confession, and reflection upon the truth of the resurrection and the powerful hope it confers.

Despite its clear benefits, we seldom take advantage of hospice. In one study of over two hundred thousand cancer patients eligible for hospice care through Medicare, only 20 percent pursued such services before death.[6] When we do seek hospice, we often decide upon it too late, after illness has already gravely impaired us. Fifty-five percent of participants enroll in hospice less than a month before death,[7] despite research demonstrating worse quality of life and greater dissatisfaction among caregivers of those in hospice for less than thirty days.[8]

Although insurance coverage issues and delays in physician referrals contribute to hospice underutilization, these statistics also warn of our own inclination to pursue futile care. In general, a life expectancy of six months or less makes us eligible for hospice. Reaping the benefits of hospice requires we *acknowledge* this prognosis and accept that death is near—a reality few of us face willingly. As we explored in the beginning, however, as Christians we cling to the hope that *death is not the end.* Our faith in Christ assures us of a restoration of our bodies and a new order where no sickness, infirmity, or death blots the glory of God's creation (Rev. 21:4). Silhouetted against this promise, our frantic strivings with contraptions that rob us of moments with those we love seem all the more futile, a chasing after the wind (Eccles. 2:11). Through hospice, medicine inches toward a standard in which it too often fails: in treating not only the failing organs, but the *person*—body, mind, and spirit—intricately woven in the image of God.

Comfort Measures

While we all yearn for the home that has shaped our memories, when critically ill we are often too sick to survive an ambulance ride home from the hospital.[9] As a result, even when treatment is futile and we discontinue aggressive interventions, many of us remain in the ICU until death.[10] To guide us through these moments, ICU physicians shift their focus from cure to comfort. In "comfort measures only" (CMO), physicians discontinue interventions that induce pain and agitation and in their place provide treatments to control symptoms. Continuous infusions of narcotics to treat pain and alleviate shortness of breath are a mainstay, as are intermittent medications to relieve anxiety.

As severe illness incapacitates our loved ones, the responsibility for decisions about comfort measures often falls on our shoulders. As with the gentleman at the start of the chapter, this burden can seem unendurable. The inappropriate but often-used term "withdrawal of care" conveys a sense of abandonment that repulses us. We worry that once organ-supporting technologies are discontinued, medical staff will lose interest in our loved ones, deserting them in their hour of most dire vulnerability.

In our consternation we may further confuse comfort measures with euthanasia or physician-assisted suicide, both unbiblical interventions that intentionally speed death (see chapter 11). More than once during discussions about comfort measures, families have folded their arms across their chests and declared to me, "No mercy killing!" With our loved ones' lives at stake, such defensiveness is expected, even laudable. However, a critical distinction between euthanasia and comfort measures is *the intent*. Euthanasia intends to end life, usually through lethal injection. Comfort measures, in contrast, seek to discontinue interventions that *prolong suffering without benefit*. In the transition to comfort care, the *underlying illness* causes death. Medicines are given to palliate symptoms, not to end life. Additionally, when a medical team approaches comfort measures properly, *care always continues*. Intensive, compassionate, and personalized medical attention never stops; its focus only shifts away from aggressive and futile technology and toward peacefulness as death nears. ICU nurses are trained to perceive signs of distress. During the last hours, they remain at the bedside continuously to assess a dying patient's needs and to adjust infusions.

Even so, in the United States, ICU staff vary in their capabilities to provide comfort measures to the satisfaction of families.[11] Should any concerns arise, we should feel empowered to *ask questions* and to request a consultation with a palliative care specialist skilled in the prevention and relief of suffering during severe illness. Although they provide recommendations at all stages of disease, palliative care physicians have extensive experience in death and dying. In fact, their involvement at the end of life so improves quality of care in the ICU that national organizations have developed guidelines to promote their consultation.[12] As we endeavor to care for our loved ones, as Christ loved us (John 13:34–35), discussions with clergy and physicians from multiple disciplines—including palliative care—are paramount to ensure optimal care and to guard against doubt, suffering, and regret.

What to Expect with Hospice

If you recognize the advancing twilight before critical illness claims you, hospice may equip you with the support to finish life in faith, peace, and service. In hospice, a team of practitioners meets with you to discuss your most troublesome symptoms and to devise a regimen to control them. Even more importantly, physicians and nurses discuss matters most important to you: your goals at the end of life and whether you can attain key aims in the remaining time. Our aims can evolve as time passes; hospice staff will reassess your situation frequently to help you live your days meaningfully. As your disability worsens, support increases. Staff also educate family members on what to expect as death nears and provide teaching and emotional support throughout.

Even with the comprehensive support of hospice, death can scare us as it approaches. In a tragic scenario all too familiar to emergency medicine clinicians, a hospice patient who has lovingly and peacefully lived out her last weeks at home suddenly arrives in the emergency department intubated and with CPR in progress. Even with education and hospice support, we can panic when death looms. Hospice staff encourage us to call them in the event of a worsening medical condition; however, fear can compel us to call 911 instead. In such scenarios, even when we elect to focus on meaningful time in our final days, we can suffer painful medical treatments in vain and ultimately die in the hospital.

What to Expect in the ICU

As we consider our advance directives (chapter 12), we need to remember that intensive-care technology, although it can preserve life in the right circumstances, can rob us of speech and mental clarity at the end of life. When patients transition to comfort measures in the ICU, they rarely have opportunities to communicate. Final conversations with loved ones or time spent in prayer to reconcile ourselves to God seldom occur. This lack of closure can strip all involved of their resolve and hope. It can steal from us the opportunity to examine the trajectory of our lives, settle unfinished issues, heal fractured relationships, and set our eyes upon the new heavens and the new earth (Isa. 65:17; 2 Pet. 3:13).

In comfort measures, nurses stop all blood draws and other maneuvers that cause pain. Pressors and other cardiovascular medications are discontinued, as is dialysis. For those of us on minimal ventilator support, the endotracheal tube is often removed to maximize comfort and permit communication. When we require high levels of ventilator support, however, approaches vary. Death can occur rapidly after tube removal if we depend upon the ventilator for survival, and in some cases continuing the ventilator but reducing its settings to improve comfort may avoid traumatic air hunger at the end of life. In other cases, physicians prescribe sufficient doses of medications to alleviate distress after tube removal, enabling discontinuation of the ventilator even in severe respiratory failure.

Oftentimes ICU staff lift certain visiting restrictions for those receiving comfort measures, allowing family members to remain in the room for as long as they choose. Nurses turn off all monitors and alarms in the room, although such screens continue to project at the nursing stations so that clinicians may respond to any changes indicative of pain, fear, or agitation.

Key symptoms that surface as death nears are pain, anxiety, and shortness of breath. Difficulty breathing occurs as levels of acid rise in the bloodstream, compelling us to breathe faster to clear carbon dioxide and restore a normal acid-base balance. To guard against such distress, physicians often prescribe a morphine infusion. Morphine not only treats pain but also slows breathing and relieves the sensation of breathlessness. Nurses carefully monitor not only any signs of pain but also quickened breathing and will fine-tune the infusion accordingly.

In the ICU, people near death often suffer from delirium and somnolence, and families may fear that narcotic infusions will lethally sedate their loved ones. Although morphine does sedate, rarely does an infusion quicken death.[13] Unlike cases of physician-assisted suicide, in comfort measures the aim of narcotics is to *palliate symptoms, not to speed demise.*

In the final hours and minutes before the end, patients adopt unusual breathing patterns that can unsettle us. They lapse into cycles of deep, sometimes rapid breathing followed by a period of shallow breaths, and then up to two minutes without taking a breath. Patients may gasp as these cycles recur, and secretions in the upper airway can create an alarming rattling sound.

Reading about such symptoms is disturbing, but it might be comforting to know that they occur when death draws very close and the patient is already unconscious. While to onlookers we may appear to gasp for air, in fact we are drawing close to our Savior.

Out of the Depths I Cry to You

As our bodies fail, we need to lean ever more fervently upon God—our rock, our salvation, the edifice upon which we rest our hopes (Ps. 18:2). Lord willing, we recognize our own mortality before it seizes us and enjoy days still rich with God's workmanship, seek him prayerfully, and continue to serve him with our remaining breath (Phil. 1:22–26). Open and frequent dialogue with clergy and with primary doctors about our goals can aid us in living well while we can and in seeking hospice if eligible.

For those of us who spend our last days surrounded by the unfamiliar, and for the loved ones whom we leave behind, hope in Christ Jesus is all the more precious. However terrible the toils of this world, and however gravely death's shadow unsettles us, the Lord remains steadfast in his love for us (Ps. 136:1). While our time in this world crumbles away, we rest assured of the promise of a new heavens and a new earth, when the calamity of disease no longer reigns (Rev. 21:4). Death does not signal the end. Not even its sting can separate us from the love of God through Christ (Rom. 8:38–39).

Take-Home Points

- When medical interventions at the end of life threaten to harm rather than help, goals of treatment shift from cure to comfort.

- Those who are terminally ill may be eligible for hospice. In hospice care, an interdisciplinary team assists patients with the goal of maximizing quality of life as death nears.

- Hospice care often allows patients to spend their last days at home and is associated with better quality of life, less caregiver grief, and improved survival in some cases.

- Critically ill patients near death usually cannot survive an ambulance ride home to initiate hospice care. In these situations, ICU physicians, in collaboration with loved ones, transition care goals from cure to comfort measures only.

- In comfort measures, all treatments that inflict pain or discomfort are discontinued, and medications are given to treat pain and anxiety.

- The decision to shift to comfort measures only can strike caregivers with regret, guilt, and grief, with long-lasting impact. Patients often cannot participate in decision making themselves and rarely communicate with loved ones when they die in the ICU.

11

PHYSICIAN-
ASSISTED SUICIDE

With its recent sweep in legalization, physician-assisted suicide (PAS) promises to confront us with increasing frequency in the coming years. As medical technology wrenches dying from the home and commits so many to a long, debilitating end, the permissibility of assisting in death as an act of mercy has become woven into the public consciousness. Just as prayerful consideration of organ-supporting measures can better equip us to tackle end-of-life dilemmas, so also can an examination of PAS from both medical and biblical standpoints prepare us to respond to the issue in the light of the gospel.

Defining Terms

Controversy over assisted death broils over two practices: voluntary active euthanasia (VAE) and physician-assisted suicide (PAS). In VAE, at a patient's request a medical practitioner administers a lethal dose of medication, usually via IV injection, to speed dying. In PAS, physicians prescribe a lethal dose of pills, usually a powerful anti-seizure medication that deeply sedates, for a patient to ingest in his own timing.

Although some countries in Europe have embraced VAE, it remains illegal throughout the US. Debate about PAS, however, currently rages. As of September 2018, PAS is legal in California, Colorado, the District of Columbia, Montana, Oregon, Vermont, and Washington State. One in 5.5 people in the United States has access to PAS practices.[1]

Most states limit consideration of PAS to terminally ill people with a life expectancy of less than six months—the same eligibility criteria for hospice care. In Oregon, the state with the longest history of legal PAS, since 1997 1,127 people have died after ingesting lethal doses of medications prescribed by physicians.[2]

Nebulous Ethics

Before I knew Christ, I had compelling reasons to advocate for physician-assisted suicide. When I was a child, one of my relatives developed a debilitating disease that attacked the nerves controlling his muscles. The condition traps its victims within a paralyzed body, even while they remain aware and mentally sharp. Over time, he lost his ability to speak and relied upon a handheld keyboard to communicate in a robotic voice. He could no longer smile or dress himself, and fits of choking seized him when he attempted to eat. As a fiercely brilliant and aloof man who prized his self-sufficiency, over time his loss of independence fractured his spirit. His wife recounted with tears how they would embrace at random in the hallway or after she helped him to eat or dress. Such embraces occur regularly in many families, but for this couple, it was a new phenomenon, a green shoot of tenderness breaking through as witness to their grief.

One morning, while his wife was out, he laid a black plastic tarpaulin out upon the lawn of their backyard. He lay down among the birds and the trees he had so admired over the years. Then he raised a gun and took his own life.

While his death sent us reeling, a stack of letters on the kitchen table revealed the detail with which he'd calculated his end. The first note alerted his wife to call 911. In the remaining sheaves he recounted his fondest memories of bringing new babies home from the hospital. At the close of one of the letters, in a shaky scrawl that remained emblazoned upon my mind as I donned my white coat and recited the Hippocratic oath years later, he wrote the words, "Support Kevorkian."[3]

Over the ensuing years, as I witnessed the suffering that welled up from every corner of the hospital, I would remember that letter and sympathize with proponents of PAS. I would recognize the same stifling despondency in my own patients that compelled my relative to end his life. Like PAS proponents I would wonder, *Isn't there a better way? Are we really demonstrating beneficence and justice and mercy as doctors when we so thrust people into suffering that suicide seems their best option?*

Compassion for Choices, the oldest nonprofit organization in America that advocates for PAS, writes in their introductory materials, "Our vision is a society where people receive state-of-the art care and a full range of choices for dying in comfort, dignity, and control."[4] Who wouldn't agree with comfort, dignity, and control? Who would argue against compassion and choice at the end of life? Advocates of PAS assert that we all have a right to self-determination, including control over the circumstances of our death. When terminal illness strips people of the capacity to pursue life meaningfully, they argue, compassion and respect dictate that physicians honor requests to facilitate a peaceful death.

Despite my sympathies with such arguments, as I hustled through the hospital before dawn each morning during my training to change dressings, listen to lungs, and field questions among those in my charge, I could never envision myself prescribing my patients pills with the intent of ending their lives. The abstract theory of PAS seemed appealing; the practical execution did not. As it happens, others share my hesitancy. Multiple surveys over the previous decades show that only half of US physicians support PAS.[5] The American Medical Association condemns the practice in its code of medical ethics, stating, "Physician-assisted suicide is fundamentally incompatible with the physician's role as a healer, would be difficult or impossible to control, and would pose serious societal risks."[6] Skeptics warn that the imbalance of power between physician and patient exposes the dying to abuse and coercion.[7]

Even in the public sector, PAS generates confusion and uneasiness. In a 2012 Gallup survey, 64 percent of respondents agreed that doctors should be permitted to painlessly end a terminally ill patient's life upon request.[8] However, when the phrasing of the question was changed to include the term *suicide*, support dropped by 10 to 15 percent.[9] This jarring change of opinion with substitution of a single word captures both the confusion PAS engenders and the ethical dubiousness fundamental to its debate.

Compassionate, but Unbiblical

When a tweak in semantics drastically shifts support for a life-and-death issue, we need to pay attention. Even the adversary disguises himself as an angel of light (2 Cor. 11:14). The scaffolding of any argument for PAS disintegrates when silhouetted against the Bible. "Your word is a lamp to my feet and a light to my path" (Ps. 119:105). God's Word illuminates the way for us, even through the dismal and echoing confines of the hospital corridor.

When comfort measures are employed, as we noted in the previous chapter, death may occur immediately, over the course of days and weeks, or not for months, depending upon the severity of illness. If someone survives, *we never take further actions to facilitate death* because the aim is not to end life but to palliate suffering.

PAS, in contrast, drags us back to Mount Sinai. Among the ten commandments Moses received on that mountaintop, with "the thunder and the flashes of lightning and the sound of the trumpet and the mountain smoking" (Ex. 20:18), was the clear directive,

"You shall not murder" (Ex. 20:13). Even when we soften words and disguise the issue with jargon, euthanasia violates this commandment. Although mercy and a respect for autonomy may motivate us, the *active* taking of another life, *with the explicit goal to end it*, violates God's Word. In VAE, physicians commit murder directly; in PAS, they act as accomplices.

Consider, for example, a frail women for whom I cared during my fellowship training in the ICU. She arrived in the emergency room in distress, her breathing rapid, her abdomen taut as a calfskin drum and excruciatingly painful to the touch. A surgeon rushed her to the operating room, where he found her viscera encased in tumor. The muddy yellow tint of intestinal contents stained her organs, betraying a bowel perforation, but disseminated cancer had frozen all her organs into place. The surgeon could not even manipulate her intestines to find the rupture.

She arrived in the ICU intubated and sedated. "She's going to die," her surgeon said. "It was awful. What I would do is give her a big dose of paralytic and take the tube out."

At first, I thought he was making a macabre and tasteless joke. The medication he referenced paralyzes the muscles to help ventilation, but administering "a big dose" immobilizes the diaphragm. She would be unable to breathe on her own.

Yet the surgeon's expression remained severe. "I'm serious," he said. "She shouldn't have to know she's about to die. I think the humane thing is to paralyze her and take out the tube."

Shocked, I tried to explain how this approach was out of the question. We would allow her to wake up and breathe, take the tube out, and do our best to support her in her last hours. We would treat her pain and encourage her family to remain with her.

Unconvinced, the surgeon continued to insist. This time, a colleague of mine stepped in and was far more blunt:

"Sorry, but that's murder. We're not in that business."

Discussions such as these occur rarely in medicine. I had never before debated such a request and have not since. Yet this encounter demonstrates how, when we loosen our grip upon the truth of God's Word, we can commit immoral acts with kind intentions.

On Autonomy

Modern medicine prizes self-determination as a fundamental principle guiding medical care, and arguments for PAS uphold individual autonomy as the greatest good. The human right to pursue what we deem best for our lives, proponents of PAS reason, includes control over how we die.

The Bible teaches that each of us has inherent value as an image bearer of God. Additionally, the Lord gifts us with free will and authorizes us to hold dominion over his creation (Gen. 1:26; 2:15–19). Christian principles, however, diverge from secular medical ethics on the issue of autonomy. In modern Western society, rugged individualism, and the freedoms it assumes, is a sacred virtue, the bedrock principle upon which the United States was founded. In the Bible, however, true freedom comes not from individualism but from using all we have and are *to glorify God*. From Colossians 3:17: "Whatever you do, in word or deed, do everything in the name of the Lord Jesus, giving thanks to God the Father through him."

In his first letter to the Corinthians Paul reminds us that while we remain free in Christ, the cross must temper our conduct: "You are not your own, for you were bought with a price. So glorify God in your body" (1 Cor. 6:19–20). Although God has granted us free will to steward his creation, we are to wield our freedom *in service to him*. Using it to serve ourselves leads us to break his commandments. Like Adam, we covet the premise that we can govern ourselves without limit and deny the authority of the one who blessed us with freedom in the first place.

Our God-given ability to make individual choices does not justify the active taking of life through PAS. While God endows all of us with free will, our identity in Christ compels us to exercise our autonomy *in faith*, as an instrument of service. "'All things are lawful,' but not all things are helpful. 'All things are lawful,' but not all things build up" (1 Cor. 10:23).

Options in Suffering

The emergence of PAS in courtrooms and clinics signals our failure as a society to support the dying, particularly as illness disables us. The most common reason that people cite for pursuing PAS is not intractable pain, but rather *loss of independence*. A review of data in Oregon from 1998 to 2016 revealed that 79 to 92 percent of people who committed suicide with physician assistance cited loss of autonomy, inability to engage in activities that make life enjoyable, and loss of dignity as their motivations for ending life.[10] The intractable pain we might assume at the end of life was a factor in only 25 percent of cases.[11] These alarming statistics suggest not a solution in PAS but rather a gross failure on the part of American society to uplift people with progressive and debilitating illness.

Sadly, the transfer of dying from the home to the hospital mirrors a nationwide institutionalization of the debilitated. As disease and age erode independence, the solution has been to admit our elderly to nursing homes to ensure their safety. While such facilities aim to provide compassionate care for the infirm, their performance benchmarks focus on medical details rather than on the richer nuances of living life well. Dr. Atul Gawande, endocrine surgeon and author of the book *Being Mortal*, eloquently stated the rift between medical and personal care when he testified before the Senate Special Committee on Aging in 2016:

> Care plans and quality measures for nursing homes and other settings, however, focus almost exclusively on narrow issues of

health and safety like fall prevention, management of feeding tubes, nutrition, pressure ulcers and so on. These are important. But just as, if not more important to people who need help with their needs for day-to-day living is the ability to have a say over matters like privacy, the risks they are permitted to take, when they go to bed and when they wake up, how they furnish and decorate their rooms, opportunities to pursue purposes larger than just mere existence, and who will make decisions when they cannot.[12]

Such statements illustrate that, ironically, while as a society we praise autonomy at all costs, we strip this freedom away from the wisest and most experienced among us. At times we infantilize those who have accumulated the most knowledge and memories and deprive them of the spiritual riches that infuse meaning into their days. This unsettling trend highlights the crucial importance of hospice and palliative care, initiatives that sift through the diagnoses and the labels to focus on the individual—packed with potential, aglow with memories and dreams—lurking beneath the illness.

As believers, we are called to care for those afflicted with severe illness (Matt. 25:36–40). Such support is not limited to the medical trappings of a double room with curtain dividers or a hospital bed with a plastic mattress and an alarm but extends to nurturing the heart and the mind. Christian fellowship mandates that we help the terminally ill in their quest to continue the activities that add abundance to life and to foster intimacy, trust, and togetherness such that no struggling person falls prey to the lie that he "would be better off dead."

When the disarming effects of disease strip us of dignity and drain away our hope, as Christians we turn to the hope that endures even when our bodies twist and warp. We witness a renewal in Christ that surpasses the limits of our failing minds (1 Pet. 1:3). While misery steals our voice and cripples our limbs, we cleave to the assurance of a new heavens and a new earth, when disease no longer darkens hearts. We wash ourselves in the hope of that day, when our hearts "shall rejoice in your salvation" (Ps. 13:5), when with renewed bodies and invigorated minds, we sing, "I trust in the steadfast love of God forever and ever. I will thank you forever, because you have done it" (Ps. 52:8–9).

Take-Home Points

- In physician-assisted suicide (PAS), a doctor provides a terminally ill patient with medication to end his or her own life. Although controversial, this practice is increasingly common in the US, now legal in seven states.

- Legality does not always equate with Christian morality, and PAS exemplifies this rift. Although support for PAS emphasizes compassion and patient autonomy—both honorable pursuits—these tenets do not justify killing.

- PAS differs from comfort measures in intent. The goal in PAS is to facilitate death. In comfort measures, the aim is to alleviate suffering from futile or excessively burdensome measures. In the latter, if patients survive once organ support is discontinued, no actions are taken to speed death.

- Most people who pursue PAS seek relief not from intractable pain but from dependence upon others and poor quality of life in the setting of debilitating illness. Such data highlight our inadequacy in supporting those stricken with terminal illness. As Christians, we as a community of believers have a responsibility to aid those among us facing severe illness, through hospice and other support.

12

ADVANCE CARE PLANNING

Few subjects bring conversation to a screeching halt as dramatically as musings about death. The topic strikes us with fear and casts a pall over a room upon its mere mention. Yet when we stalwartly avoid the issue, we suffer through interventions intolerable to us, cannot voice our objections, and heave the burden of our care upon loved ones without equipping them for the task.

Advance care planning aims to avoid such turmoil. An umbrella term, advance care planning encompasses all documents and processes intended to help us discern our wishes for end-of-life care and includes healthcare proxy forms to designate a surrogate decision maker, orders for life-sustaining treatment, and living wills. When approached with care, advance care planning can offer solace to our loved ones as they tackle difficult decisions on our behalf.

At the Bedside

I had never met her; I did not know her voice or the unique flash of her smile. But during a terrible ten-hour period, I plunged my hands into her bleeding abdomen three times.

A colleague had called for help in the operating room. He was peeling away a tumor from her pelvis when it tore open a tangled network of adherent vessels, releasing a tide of blood into her abdomen. When I arrived, the anesthesiologist was performing CPR, and my colleague, sweat drenching his scrub cap, was scrambling to stop the bleeding.

We packed her pelvis with gauze and transfused liters of blood. When she regained a pulse, we rushed her to the angiography suite, where radiologists attempted to control the bleeding with catheters. Their procedure dammed back the flood but did not dry it up. We explored her abdomen again, clamped and tied vessels, packed more densely. She seemed to stabilize, so we brought her to the ICU.

Still, the hemorrhage continued. When I explored her abdomen for a third time, every surface oozed with blood that had thinned to the consistency of water. Her blood could no longer clot, and her kidneys shut down. As the levels of acid in her bloodstream climbed, her heart intermittently convulsed into dangerous rhythms.

Trembling, my heart leaden with dread, I called her sister. We had already spoken several times that evening, each time with our focus on the urgent need to act. This call would be different.

"Please come in," I said, my voice unsteady. "Quickly, if you can. Please just come."

When she arrived, I immediately noticed the family resemblance: the wide-set eyes, the soft, rounded features. For a wonderfully absurd moment, I flirted with the idea that this woman who sat jingling her keys in the waiting room was my patient, that all was well, that my mind had fabricated the entire horror. But her eyes met mine, their gaze fragile with grief, and all fantasy dwindled away.

She spoke first: "You're going to tell me my sister is dying, aren't you?"

I nodded, then sat down and recounted the awful events. After only a few sentences, she held up her palm.

"She would not want all the machines you're talking about keeping her alive," she said. "Not if she's dying, and there's no hope."

"She talked with you about this?" I asked.

"Oh, so many times. We both watched our mother die a horrible death after two months in the ICU. After that, my sister filled out a living will. She made sure I had a copy." She glanced through the glass doors into the ICU. "She doesn't want any of what you're doing in there."

I nodded and waited while she stared for a few moments at the floor. When she spoke again, her voice was cracking. "Can I be with her, when you let her go?" she asked.

"Of course. And you can stay as long as you need." I reached out and placed my hand on her arm, as my own tears broke through. "I'm so sorry that this happened. I'm sorry we couldn't save her."

She bit her lip, wiped her eyes. "I know, I know you've done all you could," she said kindly. "I just don't want her to suffer. She was so clear about this kind of thing. If God's calling her home, she doesn't want us getting in the way." Her eyes met mine again. "I don't want to lose my sister. But at least I don't have any doubt about what she would want."

Why Participate in Advance Care Planning?

This case scenario offers an example of how advance care planning can guide those we love through heartbreaking circumstances. The power of this process to protect is not just hypothetical. In one study of four thousand people at the end of life, care decisions rested upon the shoulders of loved ones in nearly half of cases.[1] Research shows that in such circumstances, advance care planning protects against care that contradicts our values, guides physicians and caregivers when death nears, and prevents futile and aggressive treatment that prolongs dying.[2] Furthermore, studies reveal less depression, anxiety, and stress among loved ones when we provide instructions for them ahead of time.[3]

As Christians, advance care planning has even deeper value. The focus on our final days permits us to prayerfully consider our lives and to seek after the Lord as our narrative draws to its conclusion. It allows us to echo the psalmist, who declares: "I will meditate on your precepts and fix my eyes on your ways" (Ps. 119:15). The process offers a window for spiritual preparation, to lay up for ourselves treasures in heaven (Matt. 6:20). With the span of our lives receding behind us, the memories crowding together like cobblestones, we can offer up praise for his mercies and thanks for his blessings and pray about the shadows that linger, the dark hollows that remain unfilled in our hearts. We can intentionally focus on God's saving work through Christ, our reconciliation, and the facets of our lives through which we can more fully honor him. We can embrace Paul's directive: "Whatever you do, work heartily, as for the Lord and not for men, knowing that from the Lord you will receive the inheritance as your reward. You are serving the Lord Christ" (Col. 3:23–24). Advance care planning, even while it may unnerve us, grants us an avenue for worship through faithful discernment before catastrophe wrenches speech, thought, and prayer from us. When we embrace advance care planning with our minds on heaven, the process evolves into an ongoing dialogue rather than remaining an awkward and unwelcome hurdle to overcome.

Introduction to Advance Care Planning

Documentation in advance care planning focuses on two key areas: surrogacy and care preferences. Phrased more simply:

1. Who will make decisions for me if illness incapacitates me?
2. Which approaches to treatment are consistent with my goals and which are not?

Most advance care planning forms address these two questions.

As we consider a daunting array of documentation, we may fear that such measures will limit our freedom and bind us to a fate to which we may later object. However, advance directives intend not to constrain our choices but give us a voice when illness claims our ability to speak for ourselves. We should regularly reappraise our care goals as our baseline health status improves or deteriorates to protect against treatment at odds with our values.[4]

Legal documentation varies between states, and the array of options can confuse those of us already struggling with difficult issues. Although the forms themselves provide crucial instructions in the event of our incapacitation, *contemplation and candid discussion* matter most. Conversations with trusted doctors, pastors, and family to work out our convictions carry more import than does any individual checkbox form.

In the following discussion, we will review the major categories of advance directives. Appendix 2 provides links to resources on state-specific documentation, and reference to these sites will provide details unique to your state of residence. The appendix also includes a draft of my own living will, offered as an example.

Healthcare Proxy

A healthcare proxy, also called a healthcare durable power of attorney, legally designates whom physicians should consult for medical decisions on our behalf when we cannot communicate. The form usually denotes a primary surrogate decision maker and a secondary backup. Proper documentation requires signatures from all involved parties, i.e., from you, from one or two surrogates, and from two witnesses.

Without a healthcare proxy on file, physicians will still seek out your family for guidance, giving your spouse first priority, followed by your children. Although law does not *require* a proxy form, official designation avoids conflict and uncertainty within families and opens the channels of communication, promoting an exchange of thoughts regarding what matters to you most in life. Not only does this process protect you against unwanted treatments, but it ameliorates the guilt, stress, and doubt that your loved ones shoulder when critical illness claims your speech.[5]

When we appoint someone we love to assume our voice and couple that designation with in-depth conversations, *the hard decisions remain ours*, not theirs. Families who designate a surrogate and discuss wishes ahead of time often voice relief. "I know this is what he would have wanted," they say. "This is so hard to do, but at least I know I'm honoring his wishes."

When designating a healthcare proxy, carefully consider who will best weather the emotional storm that end-of-life decisions unearth. Once charged with the responsibility of acting on your behalf, your healthcare proxy may need to make decisions that conflict with his or her own preferences.[6] Carefully consider, therefore, whom God has equipped for the task.

Physician Orders for Life-Sustaining Treatment

Over the past decade, a nationwide initiative has promoted "physician orders for life-sustaining treatment" (POLST). The POLST program aims to protect us against unwanted interventions in *emergency* settings through a standardized checkbox form that documents preferences for specific interventions, including resuscitation, ventilation, and hospital transfer. You or your surrogate signs the form, as does a treating physician, ideally after extensive discussion about end-of-life care.

POLST forms quickly and clearly communicate preferences for life-sustaining treatment when time is crucial and especially protect against unwanted treatment during transfers between facilities, when communication can be chaotic.[7] Emergency responders, e.g., paramedics, emergency medical technicians, police officers, and fire department workers, are trained to look for the form when providing medical aid to you in your home.

The usefulness of POLST forms hinges on their simplicity. They declare in clear, unambiguous terms whether emergency responders should intubate us and perform CPR. The streamlined approach of these forms, however, also creates drawbacks, as they do not permit an elaboration of our values in nuanced terms.

Given the limitations, I would recommend against completing a POLST form until your chronic medical conditions become debilitating or life threatening.[8] For example, when enrolled in hospice for untreatable cancer, or when struggling daily with worsening end-stage heart disease, CPR and intubation can inflict clear harm. In these scenarios, POLST forms can protect you. On the other hand, when your list of medical conditions is limited to well-controlled hypertension and diabetes, with treatment options readily available and with a further life expectancy of years, POLST forms provide little help. In fact, such a categorical approach may create arbitrary dividing lines in moments that call instead for discernment and discussion. When doubt persists about whether to complete a POLST form, I strongly encourage in-depth discussion with your doctor.

Living Wills

Living wills outline treatment preferences, as do POLST forms; however, they are not limited to checkbox items. They often include space for narrative exposition of values and prompts about specific concerns. For example, the living will form for the state of Alabama includes fields to discuss terminal illness and permanent unconsciousness, as well as artificially administered nutrition. Forms from New York and Oregon include sections that address intolerable pain. Such details provide doctors and loved ones with vital guidance when you cannot communicate your wishes. All advance directive documents can help, but of the options we have discussed, when completed carefully the living will is the most expansive and informative.

Unlike POLST forms, you can complete a living will without a physician's authorization, although most forms require signatures from witnesses. To view your state-approved forms for living wills and other advance directives, visit the National Hospice and Palliative Care Organization (NHPCO) website. Another helpful tool is the Five Wishes program, a living will template that elaborates end-of-life preferences in plain language. Web addresses for NHPCO and Five Wishes appear in the Further Reading section in the back of the book.

Reflecting upon Our Days

The most helpful advance directive I've ever read used no official forms. As my team and I agonized over worsening vital signs, a family member dropped a packet of stapled pages into my hands. The narrative detailed the moments in my patient's life that he most treasured and the ideals that had fueled his days. As I read his words, my patient's personality and convictions, which his illness had screened from me, unfolded in vibrant strokes on the pages. Although he hypothesized about various medical scenarios, his reflections revealed, most importantly, *who he was* and *what mattered to him*. His medical conclusions seemed inevitable, the only conceivable ending to a well-crafted story.

Such attention to principles has enormous value. Advance directives are a tool. The predominant merit of advance directives resides not in their technicalities but in the conversations they promote and the guidance they convey. Rarely can we predict every possible medical calamity that might befall us. While we should carefully consider the potential risks we face, we are foolhardy to tackle a laundry list of diagnoses without binding them together with unifying principles. Statements of our beliefs as Christians can help. Additionally, clear and simple examples of the moments when our lives bloom with meaning contrasted with moments that hobble us in suffering can help to guide others when we cannot speak for ourselves. Contemplating the intricacies of our lives— our values, our worth in Christ, our memories and hopes—and sharing our conclusions with those dear to us, casts light upon otherwise grim situations. It throws open a door through which sunlight can filter, chasing away the shadows and the cobwebs.

One story provides an example. A few years ago I oversaw the care of a severely debilitated woman who struggled through complications in the ICU for months. The longer she stayed, the more infections she developed. Soon illness had emptied her of all strength, and even during brief moments of improvement she could barely lift her head from a pillow without assistance.

We met with her family multiple times over the course of her ICU stay, and they voiced concerns that she might not consent to ongoing treatments if she could speak for herself. Nurses further noticed her discouragement and predicted she might request comfort measures if asked.

When we sat down with her during a period of lucidity, she surprised us all. In a voice we could barely hear, and with a tremulous finger upraised, she identified the thing most important to her: the ability to watch television with her family. She wished to press on, through the staggering setbacks, the mounting infections, and the days that slogged interminably, if such measures graced her with a few good stories and a familiar pat on the arm. Commonplace companionship was more precious to her than the independence and comforts her treatments had long ago abolished. She guided us to continue aggressive care in the weeks that followed, past points that others would have expected. Eventually, she regained enough stability to transfer to a rehabilitation center, where she continued to watch TV shows with her family at her side.

On Autonomy

As we discussed in the previous chapter, protection of individual self-determination is a driving force in medical ethics. As image bearers of God, we indeed possess inherent dignity and free will. Our capacities to create and to innovate reflect God's goodness, with our choices for righteousness shimmering ripple-like through the expanse of human history. Yet, as Christians, we know that God grants us freedom not for self-aggrandizement *but for his glory*. Our worth stems from Christ, not from our rugged individualism. When we cling to our autonomy at the expense of all other principles, we slink toward idolatrous self-reliance. The question "What would I want?" does not encompass all our concerns as we consider end-of-life care. Rather, as we remember God's work, his weaving and refining of our steps as we journey toward heaven, we must ask ourselves, "How can I continue to faithfully serve God?"

As we consider our walk in faith at the end of life, we must remember that endotracheal tubes, sedation, and critical illness strip us of speech and alertness. While a ventilator breathes for us and medications fog our mind, we can neither pray nor confess nor seek out life-giving fellowship with others. If these measures promise to return us home, where we may live out our faith, the discomforts and dependence may be worthwhile. On the other hand, if we pursue such interventions in the face of futility, technology can eliminate our abilities to pray and reflect in the moments when we most need to lean upon God.

On Suffering

Suffering does not conform to a universal mold. Our experience of suffering and our steadiness as we pilot its swells depend upon the unique circumstances, temperaments, and histories that shape us. Our lives evolve in patchwork, with each fragment, each memory, either reinforcing our forbearance or fraying against the wind.

As with my patient who was content to endure pain and disability if she could watch television with family, some of us have a high threshold for discomfort and harvest deep joy from simplicity. For others who smolder within the crucible of suffering, even marginal deficiencies in independence may shatter the soul. As we outline our wishes for the end of life, we must be honest: what can we endure, and what would irrevocably drown us in despair?

Scripture teaches us that hardship riddles the path of the believer (Mark 13:13; Luke 14:27; John 16:33; Rom. 8:18; 2 Tim. 3:12; 1 Pet. 4:12–19) but also that God engages with suffering to enact good (Gen. 50:20; John 9:1–3; Rom. 8:28). Even while we toil through the gloom, God sees us, knows us, loves us, and draws us closer to him. "The LORD is near to the brokenhearted," writes the psalmist, "and saves the crushed in spirit" (Ps. 34:18). Also, from Romans 5:3–5:

> Not only that, but we rejoice in our sufferings, knowing that suffering produces endurance, and endurance produces character, and character produces hope, and hope does not put us to shame, because God's love has been poured into our hearts through the Holy Spirit who has been given to us.

Some suffering can refine us and deepen our faith. And yet we serve a God who abounds in love and mercy (Ex. 34:6; Pss. 86:5; 103:8). He knows each of us individually and loves us as a father cherishes his children (Pss. 46:1; 94:18–19; 147:3; Isa. 41:10; 43:1–3; Jer. 1:5). While God may engage with suffering to strengthen, discipline, and instruct us, in his mercy he does *not* condemn us to wallow in unbearable pain without purpose. As a father would not so torment his children, so God does not delight in our crushing (Lam. 3:31–33; Ezek. 33:11). He does not require us to pursue medical treatments that would ravage us.

Through it all, the saving grace of Christ Jesus offers us a living hope to sustain us (1 Pet. 1:3; Rev. 21:4). Whatever trials we bear, we cling to the assurance of our salvation in him.

Wisdom Begins with the Word

As we consider our advance directives, we must return to the biblical principles outlined in the first chapter. Gospel-centered end-of-life care requires consideration of the following precepts.

1. *Mortal life is sacred.* Our lives are a gift from God. We are made in the image of God, and each one of us has inherent dignity and value. We are to cherish and protect the life God gives us.

2. *God has authority over life and death.* This side of the fall, death escapes no one. It claims us all. While we should strive against death when there is hope of cure, to fight when such efforts are futile discounts God's steadfast love and his ability to effect

good even as our lives end. To deny our mortality is to ignore the saving grace of the gospel.

3. *We are called to love one another.* God desires for us to be merciful and compassionate. He calls us to care for the ill and to alleviate suffering. We should not compel people to doggedly chase after treatments that inflict agony. Likewise, we need not accept such interventions ourselves, if suffering overwhelms us.

4. *As followers of Christ, we need not fear death!* Even as our lives draw to a close, we cherish the promise of new life. We rest assured in Christ's sacrifice for us and in the awe-inspiring depth of God's love. Our transition into death is transient and fleeting, a momentary beating of wings. Through Christ's resurrection, we find the promise of restoration, of new life in communion at last with our everlasting God.

As we have explored throughout this book, these principles guide us to: (1) seek aggressive treatments when they offer hope of recovery but (2) decline them when they only prolong death, or when they inflict suffering without commensurate benefit. Including such language in our advance directives can help to guide caregivers when critical illness strikes us.

Guiding Questions

Although advance directives often distill medical decisions into yes/no responses, a vast middle ground spans the extremes of recovery and death. Too often, medical treatment offers not complete recovery but life with new infirmity. For example, you may survive a disastrous battle with sepsis in the ICU but spend months in rehabilitation centers, unable to walk independently or feed yourself. You may suppress leukemia with chemotherapy, but it so shatters your immune system that you spend your extra days in the hospital fighting infections. Or you may undergo life-saving intestinal surgery but not return home for a year due to a long procession of complications.

As we consider our goals of care in such circumstances, the path forward hinges on the questions of suffering upon which we have touched. How much disability are we able to bear? What would crush us? Above all, through the pain and discouragement, how do we continue to serve God? How do we understand the gospel, even as we suffer? With these concerns in mind, a few additional prompts can guide us.

1. What are my goals for the end of life?
This question pertains to how you wish to spend your final days, in light of your walk in the Spirit. Is it important to remain at home? What matters to you as your life ends? Who matters? What activities invigorate you and fasten your gaze heavenward? What places and people are most precious to you? When you envision the end of your life, what details do you most prize?

2. How can I continue to serve God at the end of life?
Think back to the moments in your life when you have reveled in the joy of the Lord. When have you felt him nearest? Consider the times you have praised him, thanked him, or endeavored to serve him. What did you require in those moments? What will you still require for faithful service as illness closes upon you?

3. How much suffering is too much?
As you envision periods of pain and dependence, what would constitute undue suffering? What outcomes are unacceptable to you, no matter the gain? What would so burden you as to strip away your ability to serve God with joy? What would be intolerable?

*4. What trials am I willing to endure to
achieve my goals at the end of life?*
What are you comfortable sacrificing, and what sacrifice would be unacceptable? As an example, if you aim to spend your final days at home with family, would you be willing to have a ventilator at home to enable this? Would you endure medical treatments that

impair consciousness to extend life, or must you be in command of your mental faculties, even if declining treatment quickens the end? Consider the interventions outlined throughout the book and strive to envision what you would be willing to endure to meet your goals at the end of life.

* * *

Statements that summarize the questions above can guide loved ones when a clinical situation falls outside the parameters of checkboxes. To illustrate this, I have included my living will in Appendix 2. I provide this only as *an example*; your advance directives should reflect your own responses to the questions above, after prayerful consideration.

To clearly outline my directives, I considered biblical principles and then answered the four questions above as follows:

1. What are my goals at the end of life?

My goals are to spend my final days of life at home, communing with family and friends. I yearn for as much time as possible in the quiet of our wooded backyard, where I spent so many evenings casting my thoughts into the twilight, and where I taught my children how to read, count, and relish adventure. God-willing, I wish to be lucid enough to spend time in prayer, reading, and reflection before my passing. I yearn for life-giving fellowship with loved ones and with other believers. I long to glorify God through the written word. Reading and writing are nourishment and air for me.

2. How can I continue to serve God at the end of life?

Through his graciousness, God has demonstrated for me time and again how we most serve him when we love one another. As long as I possess my mental faculties and power to communicate, I believe I can honor him. The powers of speech and writing—and my ability to comprehend each of these—have been vital to my walk in Christ. To serve God, I need to think, to reason, to pray, and to exchange ideas in fellowship with others.

3. How much suffering is too much?

Any debilitating, terminal illness that would permanently impair my ability to communicate is abhorrent to me. When I say "communicate," I refer not to gestures but to the lively exchange of ideas. I would not accept organ-supporting measures or artificially administered nutrition in the event of persistent coma, vegetative state, or minimally conscious state. Should I suffer from advanced dementia such that I can no longer vouch for myself, I wish for continued loving care and feeding by hand but no aggressive measures. In particular, I would decline CPR, mechanical ventilation, artificially administered nutrition, or dialysis in this setting.

4. What trials am I willing to endure to achieve my goals at the end of life?

I would be willing to accept organ-supporting technology for the above conditions if physicians held out a significant chance of improvement, such that I might regain my ability to communicate. I would be willing to endure prolonged ventilator dependence, paralysis, dependence upon others for activities of daily living, and other debilitating conditions *presuming that treatments promised to restore my abilities to reason, to exchange ideas, and to engage in fellowship with others.* Communication and thought are key to my walk in faith.

* * *

These responses formed the basis of the living will that appears in the appendix. Your advance directives may diverge markedly from mine and should reflect your unique medical situation, life story, and relationship with God.

I would encourage all drafting an advance directive to *talk openly with physicians* and to *readily ask questions.* Frequent and candid dialogue with a pastor can also be life-giving during such heavy deliberations. Finally, as I have emphasized throughout this chapter, in advance care planning the documents help but they comprise only *one component* of a profoundly important process. Conversations and open communication with loved ones, especially those who may have to make decisions for us, guard against anguish as we set our eyes upon Jesus.

Take-Home Points

- Advance care planning refers to the process of outlining our wishes for end-of-life care and communicating these preferences with our doctors and family.

- Advance directives are legal documents that record our preferences. Forms include a healthcare proxy to designate a surrogate decision maker, physician orders for life-sustaining treatment, and living wills.

- All advance directive documents intend to provide guidance to our family and caregivers in the moments when critical illness impairs our ability to make decisions. Studies show that advance care planning alleviates anxiety and stress among loved ones and protects against unwanted treatments and hospitalizations.

- The most important feature of advance care planning involves no form but rather revolves around the *process*. Deliberating our wishes for end-of-life care and communicating these with our family are paramount.

- As Christians, our consideration of end-of-life care should focus on faithful service to God.

13

BEING A VOICE

Surrogate Decision Making

Throughout this book, I have addressed questions of end-of-life care with loved ones in mind, because in the arena of aggressive ICU technology, the burden of decision making so frequently falls upon families. Many of us will find ourselves in a conference room against our wishes, wringing our hands, wondering what to do for someone whom we cannot fathom losing. Sadly, many of us will be compelled to make crushing decisions while grief drowns us.

At the Bedside
"He would never have wanted this."

With one hand she wiped tears from her eyes, and with the other she gripped her father's mottled fingers. She glanced at her mother and brother, both brooding in the room with her, then returned to brush hair from her father's forehead. His gaunt face, the eyes half open and vacant, contrasted with collages of photographs on the walls that depicted him golfing, or laughing as he clutched a tow-headed grandchild to his chest. In one picture he stood with a robust arm around his wife and beamed as she nestled into him.

"Mom," his daughter said, turning to that same wife, who in grief had also become a dwindling shadow of the person in the pictures. "You know he wouldn't want any of this." She motioned to the array of machinery keeping him alive: the ventilator hissing and sighing. The dialysis machine hulking at the foot of the bed. The catheters snaking into his wrist and his neck, with puncture sites oozing blood in rivulets.

"I know, Baby," his wife replied, her words barely audible.

"He wouldn't want any of this if it wouldn't bring him home," his daughter said. "He wouldn't want to needlessly suffer."

His wife never lifted her eyes but nodded vigorously. "I know."

"So, isn't it time we just let him go?" Their eyes met, and they exchanged a knowing gaze. "When his nurse comes back, let's ask to talk to the doctors."

Suddenly the patient's son, who until then had listened wordlessly in a chair with his arms crossed, raised his hand: "Knock it off, please. I'm not okay with this talk. Any of it."

"What do you mean?" his mother asked.

"What do I mean? You're talking about killing Dad."

"We're not talking about *killing him*," his sister shot back. "What a horrible thing to say! We're talking about the fact that Dad never wanted *any* of this. He's suffered a horrible stroke and now needs machines just to survive. The neurologists say he won't get better. He *told* us never to let him live like this. When do we say enough is enough?"

"Dad wouldn't give up on any of us," he insisted.

"Please," his mother pleaded, "He's suffered so much. Don't make him go through more. He doesn't want any of this. He told us. You know that."

"So we just give up on him? Is that what he would do for us?"

166

"He's dying!"

"That's for God to decide, Ma. Not us."

He bolted from his chair and stormed from the room, and his mother buried her face in her hands.

Asking the Impossible

My patient's sudden illness forced a reality upon his family that they were unprepared to face. A storm of emotions buffeted them, the subtleties of which no single meeting with a stranger could ever unearth. It thrust them into a nightmare, and they thrashed for escape, as anyone would. Grief requires time. It needs to breathe, to flow out in slow tides that heal in their wake. Yet critical illness rarely affords such space.

In one study of people over sixty, 70 percent had no capacity to make decisions for themselves at the end of life.[1] Other research echoes these findings, showing that surrogates make care decisions for people at the end of life in up to 75 percent of cases.[2]

A Burden upon the Heart

Making end-of-life decisions for loved ones takes a heavy toll on the heart, crippling many with guilt and doubt for years afterward.[3] Advance directives can assuage guilt, but when end-of-life care remains a taboo subject within a family, the risks of our silence include the brutality of unwanted treatment and the imprisonment of regret. Even when God blesses us with a clear path, the ramifications of walking the road can haunt us for years afterward. "Luckily, I knew what her wishes were," a friend recounted to me after her mother's death. "But watching her die over the course of two days was unbelievably heart wrenching." Death originates in sin. Even when we guard ourselves with discussions and advance directives, its impact shakes us to our bones and casts a shadow over our hearts that can linger long after we have said goodbye.

While striving to make the "right" choices, we need to acknowledge the depth of our own turmoil. Given the stakes, the grief and agony we experience are expected. Recognize the need for gentleness. Create leeway for sorrow. Pray. Reach out. When darkness penetrates our days and impossible decisions suffocate us, fellowship reminds us of our hope in Christ, enfolds us in love, and bolsters us with life-giving courage. "If we walk in the light, as he is in the light, we have fellowship with one another, and the blood of Jesus his Son cleanses us from all sin" (1 John 1:7). Seek support. Reach out to family, to chaplaincy, to your church. Surround yourself with the love of Christ to guard your heart and to spur you on.

Not Our Voice, but Theirs

Surrogate decision making requires that we differentiate our loved ones' preferences from our own desires. Your role as a healthcare proxy is not to answer what *you* would do, or even what you want for your loved one. Rather, your task is to discern *how he would choose for himself*. In other words, your goal is to be the voice of the patient, to answer as he would if he still possessed the power to speak. This process, called "substituted judgment," requires us to step outside of our own wants, to put aside the strife churning within us, and to contemplate the unique attributes of those for whom we care. It mandates setting aside our yearning to embrace a loved one again and focusing instead on the values and experiences that clarify his approach to the world.

Studies show that we often miss the mark. One systematic review revealed that next-of-kin surrogates accurately predict a patient's preferences in only one-third of cases.[4] Interestingly, in this study advance directives did *not* improve predictive accuracy. In other words, even when patients had communicated their preferences, surrogates made decisions contrary to their wishes. Communication happened, but something broke down in translation. Such data warn against making decisions hastily, according to our own incentives. As surrogates, our role is to honor our loved ones as unique image bearers of God. With dignity comes the freedom to make choices about care, in stewardship of our God-granted bodies (1 Cor. 6:19–20; Phil. 1:20).

As we discussed in the previous chapter, Christian autonomy intertwines with the gospel. The Bible disallows us to take our own lives or to willingly take that of another. However, how we serve God with our gifts and how we experience suffering are highly individualistic. To love one another as Christ has loved us requires that we view one another as God sees us: cherished, forgiven, wonderfully made, and *unique*, with no precise equal on earth (see Ps. 139:13–14; John 3:16; Rom. 8:35; Eph. 1:7). Such a view requires that we look past our own desperation for a loved one to remain with us always; examine the special traits that constitute his temperament, personality, and dreams; and accept wherever that inquiry leads us—even if we ourselves deplore the outcome. For the family at the beginning of this chapter, this approach meant acknowledging that their loved one abhorred medicine, prized independence, and would never have consented to the interventions with which we barraged him.

Questions to Ask

Surrogate decision making, while impossibly difficult, permits us to live out the commandment to love our neighbors as ourselves. It requires us to set aside our wants and concerns and to seek after the minds and hearts of those we love. Although the burden threatens to crush us, when we persevere in love and faithfulness to support our loved ones in their last days, we live out the gospel. We embrace a truth that triumphs over death.

When seated at the conference table, if no advance directives exist, a series of questions can help guide us. As we have discussed throughout this book, the first task is to determine whether treatment promises recovery or only prolongation of suffering and death. We return to the questions introduced in chapter 2:

- What is the condition that threatens my loved one's life?
- Why is the condition life-threatening?
- What is the likelihood for recovery?
- How do my loved one's previous medical conditions influence his or her likelihood for recovery?
- Can the available treatments bring about cure?
- Will the available treatments worsen suffering, with little chance of benefit?
- What are the best and worst expected outcomes?

If these questions point to a high likelihood for recovery, pursuing treatment makes sense. However, if illness has so critically progressed that tubes, medicines, and machines promise suffering without clear hope for recovery, we need not insist upon burdensome measures.

When the futility of treatment is ambiguous—when the prognosis is unclear or recovery possible only with significant disability—our task becomes more opaque. These moments demand that we muster the most strength, patience, and insight, even while our sorrow ill-equips us to wield such virtues. They require us to limp forward, still lame with grief, and to displace mountains.

Our chief goal must be to hear our loved one's voice. We need to discern which treatments would be too objectionable for a loved one to endure and which he would embrace despite detriment to his comfort, independence, and lifestyle. Again, as this responsibility staggers our mind, a series of questions can guide us:

- What matters most to my loved one? What drives him in life?
- What comments has he made in the past regarding end-of-life care, if any?
- What are his goals, both in the short term and for his life in general?

- What is he willing to endure to achieve those goals? What would he be unwilling to face?
- How well in the past has my loved one tolerated pain, dependence, disability, and fear?
- *If he could speak for himself, what would he say about the current situation?*

Such inquiry can anchor us when our own pain swallows our thoughts. It can also assist when disagreement arises between family members about the proper course of action. Every ICU physician can relate stories of estranged siblings or children reappearing during the final days and hours before death to object to the plan of care. Such scenarios point to the complexity and messiness of end-of-life discussions; they rarely occur neatly packaged but rather simmer with mottled histories and buried sentiments. The goal, without fail, is to *focus on what our loved one would say.* These debates should center not on ourselves but on the one whose voice we strive to adopt.

These questions can especially help when we vouch for loved ones who are not believers. Doubts about our beloved's salvation can further grieve us when we navigate unfamiliar and painful territory, and we worry about how to proceed when an ill family member has never shared our values. The temptation arises in these situations to proceed as we would for *ourselves*, but such an approach does not embrace the status of our loved ones as unique image bearers of God (Gen. 1:27; Ps. 139:14–16) So long as a loved one's wishes do not violate God's law—as no practice within the hospital should—we must honor their thoughts on suffering and medically prolonged death.

The responsibility as surrogate decision makers can seem too arduous to withstand. Yet when we aim to hear our loved one's voice after it has fallen silent, we honor and love him. In so doing, we also serve God the Father, who gave his Son to secure our loved one a home in heaven.

171

Grief in the Aftermath

The impact of deciding upon our loved ones' care can linger for years afterward and strike many of us with depression, complicated grief, anxiety, and guilt.[5] The pain from the initial loss can chisel away at our souls long after we have said goodbye. "I think of her every day, and I ask God to forgive me for not protecting her," one mother confided in me, after losing her daughter. Guilt shatters our concentration and disturbs our dreams. Sorrow weighs us down. Atop this grief, as we consider our loved ones' struggles before death, we may feel unworthy of our sadness.

When our deceased loved one was not a believer, our uncertainty about his or her salvation can further torment us. While few words can assuage this pain, we find comfort in the narrative of the penitent criminal crucified beside Jesus (Luke 23:40–43). With his dying breath, this sinner confessed faith in Jesus and secured a position alongside him in Paradise. While we cannot know the full depth and complexity of our loved one's heart and thoughts, we *can* be assured of God's grace, his mercy, and his goodness (Gen. 18:14, 25; Ex. 34:6). We cannot know our loved one's fate, but we cling to the Lord's abundant mercy.

God knows our pain. He draws near to us as we cry out in anguish (Ps. 34:18). We need not run from our sorrow or fear weeping. From a biblical standpoint, the only initial response to sadness—to the broken matters of a world wrenched from God's perfection—is lamentation.

In the garden of Gethsemane, as he anticipated the cross, Jesus was "very sorrowful, even to death," and "being in agony he prayed more earnestly; and his sweat became like great drops of blood falling down to the ground" (Matt. 26:38; Luke 22:44). Jesus also wept when Lazarus died. He knew the Father would empower him to reanimate Lazarus from death. He had absolute assurance in the Father's authority and goodness. Yet when faced with the death of a friend, he wept, prompting onlookers to remark, "See how he loved him!" (John 11:33–36).

That Christ himself wept illuminates the importance of grief. Christ wept out of love. When we open ourselves to the outcries of our heart, we proclaim that which we mourn as precious. We declare that there exist things in this world of great worth, of meaning, of value that exceed any glimmering stone dug from the earth. We praise God both through treasuring his workmanship and lamenting its loss.

Still, when grief descends, we can grapple with strangling loneliness. When the shadows wrap you in their cold limbs, I encourage you to seek out fellowship with those who have traveled the same road. A number of Christian bereavement services aim to support those of us suffering through the aftermath of loss. The Further Reading section includes a list of such resources, in particular GriefShare, a Christian recovery support group geared toward healing.

Amidst our grief, we rest in the assurance that "the one who endures to the end will be saved," and that when Christ returns, "he will wipe away every tear" (Matt. 10:22; Rev. 21:4). Yet in the meantime, while still locked in a fallen world, we "weep with those who weep" (Rom. 12:15). We lament, and thirst for God.

Take-Home Points

- Most people cannot speak for themselves at the end of life. Often, decisions about care fall to loved ones.

- Surrogate decision making requires us to consider *how our loved one would answer*. A loved one's wishes may differ from our own, and our challenge is to embrace his or her unique attributes and preferences rather than chase after our own desires.

- A series of questions can guide us in differentiating life-prolonging from death-prolonging treatment. Additionally, inquiry can help us decipher what might constitute undue suffering for a loved one, and what he or she might be willing to endure to preserve what matters in life.

• Complicated grief, guilt, anxiety, and depression afflict surrogate decision makers in the aftermath of a loved one's passing. We are compelled neither to suffer alone nor to swallow our sorrow. Seek support from friends and believers enduring the same tribulations.

CONCLUSION

I trained in critical care out of passion for the success stories. Remembrances of the trauma victims who survived car crashes, the mothers with life-threatening sepsis whom we returned home to their children, and the gallant rescues of fathers with ruptured aortic aneurysms have inspired me and sped me on. This book does not capture such stories, but they provide ample and vivid evidence that when used well, critical care represents an instrument of God's mercy, a vehicle for his compassion.

Yet, as I hope the preceding pages have illustrated, tragedies arise when we foist these same dramatic measures upon the dying. The ICU, for all its healing potential, blurs the boundary between the heroic and the inhumane. Brittle bodies do not mend easily. When we tackle the enfeebled and the fragile with aggressive measures, we shatter that which we seek to protect. Among the terminally ill, ICU technology can actually shorten life and steal from us precious time necessary for spiritual preparation.

Modern medicine's perversion of the dying process became apparent to me thousands of miles from the ICU in which I worked. During a medical mission to Kenya, a gentleman shuffled through the schoolroom door where I sat with half a dozen other clinicians in our makeshift clinic. The cool of the early morning had burned away, and I habitually wiped sweat and red dust from my skin as I tugged off my white coat. The hours spent piecing together medical histories in clumsily translated Swahili had drained me.

He eased himself into a plastic chair. He clutched a cane for refinery, not for infirmity, and cordially removed his tattered hat when he introduced himself. Worry creased his brow.

"I was wondering if you could please help me," he said. "I had an operation for hemorrhoids some time ago, but it's not fixed anything. I am constantly bleeding. Every time I go back, they just give me tablets, but they don't help. I wish to know what I have. Even if it is something that cannot be cured, I just wish to know."

He dropped a dilapidated booklet of hospital records onto my table. I leafed through the stained pages and froze upon a word scrawled in pencil. My heart sank. He did not have hemorrhoids. He had rectal cancer. He also could not afford the operation that might save his life.

I searched his eyes, and a verse surfaced: "Your faith has made you well" (Matt. 9:22). I choked back tears, leaned forward, and held his hand. We discussed his diagnosis for the next half hour. I drew diagrams. We prayed together.

After we spoke, he paused for a long while, deep in thought. I watched a complex parade of emotions silently dance over and then flicker away from his face. "Thank you for explaining to me," he finally said. The creases had smoothed from his forehead. While his gaze was plaintive, I saw no distress in his eyes, but only a quiet remorse. "I see you have sympathy and compassion for me, and I am grateful. I am in the Lord's hands now. I must trust in him. He will provide what is best for me."

This gentleman lived in a remote Kenyan village, hours away from any hospital. The pastor with whom we served told us stories of people carrying loved ones on mats for miles to receive medical attention, only to have them die in the road. That such disparities in medical care exist, and that they victimize the poor, exemplifies how sin still thrives while we await the return of our Savior. We contemplate them, and we cannot help but fall to our knees, gasping for breath.

My patient had no choices for further care. The trappings of intensive care were foreign and remote, not even options for him. And yet the clarity of his path—however dismaying it was—permitted him to focus on *what really mattered*. With his fate apparent, he turned in fullness of heart and faith to God.

Intensive-care technology rarely allows us such reflection. In the best scenario, we focus on the next procedure, the numbers, and the technicalities, with little reserve left to contemplate our faith. In the worst case, the technology upon which we rely so heavily hijacks our freedom to worship. It bars us from communion, fellowship, contemplation, and even prayer.

When we forfeit focus on God and his Word to chase after machines, we ignore God's grace. We worship creation rather than its maker. We discount the saving grace of the gospel and the brilliant hope of the resurrection in favor of man-made technology, forged by imperfect hands.

Yet as our grief, our fear, and our affliction surge forward to overtake us at the end of life, they still cannot threaten our hope. In all things, the cross transforms our worth, our fate, and our view of the end. We serve a God who so loves us that he gave us his Son to wipe clean our sins (John 3:16). Even when the threat of death enshrouds us, we rest in the assurance that Christ has *defeated* death and that "for those who love God all things work together for good, for those who are called according to his purpose" (Rom. 8:28). Even in our sufferings, we serve Christ (Rom. 5:3–5).

The last breath to slip from our bodies signals the end to our earthly lives but *not* the end of our walk with God. For the believer who knows and loves Christ, death loses its sting (1 Cor. 15:55) and ushers us into communion with the One who has known us since before the womb (Ps. 139:13). When Christ returns, no sickness or death will blot the new heavens and the new earth (Rev. 21:4). Our brokenness in both body and soul will heal. Our fractures will mend. Our fears will vanish. And the love of our Lord Jesus, in its blinding brilliance, will wash us in light for all eternity.

In the meantime, while we struggle with turmoil in these days, on this earth with its crumbling edifices, let us lean into our faith (Prov. 3:5–6). Let us embrace one another. Let us care for one another in truth and love. And while ventilators sigh and alarms blare, let us find our ultimate solace in the truth: "My flesh and my heart may fail, but God is the strength of my heart and my portion forever" (Ps. 73:26).

ACKNOWLEDGMENTS

Although its impression has lingered upon my heart for years, I never set out to write a book. The endeavor unfolded gradually, out of God's grace, and through the generous encouragement of mentors, friends, and a few remarkable colleagues who offered me their time and counsel despite never having met me before. The attention poured into this book is a testament to the love and generosity so central to the body of Christ.

I thank Tony Reinke and the staff at Desiring God for their encouragement with this idea, for their patience with and support of an unknown writer, and for guiding this project from its inception as an article series to the book it has become. To Pastor Jefrey Jensen at Our Savior Lutheran Church, and Dr. Bob Weise at Concordia Seminary, thank you for your keen eye and attentive feedback as I navigated the theology. I am indebted to Dr. Robert Orr for his conversations with regard to ethics and to my agent Erik Wolgemuth for his support and helpful feedback on the flow of words. I thank Dr. Justin Taylor and staff at Crossway for this opportunity, for their insight, and for their invaluable blend of professionalism and affability. A special thanks, especially, to Lydia Brownback, for her care and skill in editing this work. To my readership, so many of whom have applauded this effort, despite never having met me, I thank you heartily. To my small group and family from Our Savior, your prayers have sped me on. To my husband, Scottie, sincere thanks for tolerating my keyboard tapping at five every morning, for your steadfastness, and for the compass you are to me. To my patients over the years, thank you for the privilege to partner with you, and may God bless you. And above all, thanks be to God. May all the earth praise his name.

APPENDIX 1

Summary Chart of Organ-Supporting Measures

Intervention	Organ System(s) Supported	When It Helps	When It Hurts	Notes
CPR	Brain and heart during cardiac arrest	Immediately reversible causes of cardiac arrest, especially abnormal ventricular rhythms.	Cardiac arrest not related to a treatable heart rhythm; end-stage disease.	Causes rib fractures in most cases. Prolonged CPR associated with low survival and high incidence of brain injury.
Defibrillation	Electrical system of the heart	Life saving in lethal ventricular rhythms and some atrial arrhythmias.	Does not inflict pain during cardiac arrest, but can be painful in patients with less severe rhythms who are awake.	Defibrillation significantly improves survival.

Intervention	Organ System(s) Supported	When It Helps	When It Hurts	Notes
Endotracheal Intubation	Airway	Required to connect to a ventilator in respiratory failure; protects the airway in the event of unconsciousness, airway obstruction.	In chronic, debilitating, or terminal disease, endotracheal intubation and mechanical ventilation can prolong dying.	Associated with injury to the vocal cords and windpipe with prolonged use. Increases risk for pneumonia. Very uncomfortable; requires sedation to tolerate.
Mechanical Ventilation	Lungs	Life saving in respiratory distress, particularly for reversible causes: treatable pneumonia, fluid in the lungs from kidney or heart failure.	In chronic, debilitating, or terminal disease, endotracheal intubation and mechanical ventilation can prolong dying.	Prolonged use weakens respiratory muscles, leading to ventilator dependence. Associated with pneumonia. Often requires sedation to tolerate.
Tracheostomy	Airway, lungs	Facilitates weaning from the ventilator, and avoids injury to the vocal cords and windpipe from prolonged intubation.	Might signal a need for long-term ventilator dependence. The procedure itself carries risk of injury and bleeding.	Very helpful and temporary when respiratory failure is recoverable. If no recovery is anticipated, indicates long-term ventilator dependence.
Noninvasive Positive Pressure Ventilation (BiPAP)	Lungs	Provides support in reversible respiratory failure in conscious patients.	Not appropriate for severe or long-term respiratory failure and associated with increased mortality in such cases.	Avoids an endotracheal tube. Patients are awake and interactive. Claustrophobia may occur.

Intervention	Organ System(s) Supported	When It Helps	When It Hurts	Notes
Vasopressor and Inotropic Medications	Cardiovascular system (heart, blood pressure)	Supports the heart and blood pressure in reversible causes of shock.	High doses of pressors can restrict blood flow to the limbs and bowel, causing death of these tissues. Inotropes can cause fatal heart rhythms at high doses.	In unrecoverable critical illness, as death nears, doses lose their efficacy. A steady dose of vasopressor may not mean adequate delivery of oxygen to the organs.
Central and Arterial Lines	Cardiovascular system (for monitoring)	Allows for monitoring of vital signs continuously and administration of powerful medications. Ubiquitous in the ICU.	Lines are associated with clotting, bloodstream infection, and complications from insertion, including vessel injury and lung collapse.	Ubiquitous in the ICU but an important source of hospital-acquired infections
Artificially Administered Nutrition	Gastrointestinal system	Vital for maintaining nutrition when illness prevents normal eating.	Near death, tube feeds can cause nausea, vomiting, bloating, and cramping as the gut shuts down. In end-stage dementia, tube dislodgement and required restraints can worsen confusion and inflict suffering.	Long-term feeding through the gut requires surgical placement of a feeding tube. If the gut cannot be fed through tubes due to disease, TPN can be infused through veins, although this carries risk of infection.

Intervention	Organ System(s) Supported	When It Helps	When It Hurts	Notes
Dialysis	Kidneys	Allows survival with chronic kidney disease for as long as decades.	May significantly impair quality of life in end-stage illness.	Nephrologists offer guidelines recommending when to pursue dialysis. Need for dialysis is a marker for severe debilitating illness, and should prompt discussions about advance care planning in general.

APPENDIX 2

Sample Advance Directive

Note: I offer the following as an example. When you formulate your own advance directive, I urge you to consider your unique medical history and the facets of life pivotal to your walk of faith. Please review chapter 12 carefully. My state of residence does not legally recognize living wills and officially uses only healthcare proxy and POLST forms. As a result, I have written my living will in free form. Other states, however, have templates with prompts that can be very helpful. Please refer to the websites listed in the Further Reading section for specific links.

Living Will for Kathryn L. Butler, MD

In the event that severe illness incapacitates me, I wish for my [chief surrogate] to direct decisions in my medical care on my behalf. Should catastrophe also incapacitate him, this responsibility should fall to [secondary surrogate].

As a follower of Jesus Christ, I aim to preserve God-given life when feasible but not to ignore his authority over the extent of my life or to chase after treatments that would thwart my ability to faithfully serve him. In general, I will pursue treatments that promise recovery but not those that prolong death or those that permanently eliminate my abilities to reason and communicate.

Goals for the End of Life

- To serve God, I need to think, to reason, to pray, and to exchange ideas in fellowship with others.

- I wish to be lucid enough to spend time in prayer, reading, and reflection at the end of life.

- I yearn for life-giving fellowship with loved ones and with other believers.

- I long to glorify God through the written word. Reading and writing are nourishment and air for me.

- Any debilitating, terminal illness that would impair my ability to communicate is abhorrent to me. When I say "communicate," I refer not to gestures but to the lively exchange of ideas.

- I yearn for as much time as possible in the quiet of our wooded backyard; however, this is not essential so long as I am able to engage with others meaningfully.

- I am willing to endure physical discomfort, dependence on others, and long-term ventilator dependence if I may still exchange ideas meaningfully.

- I do not wish for aggressive, life-prolonging measures if they are futile or in the event of end-stage terminal illness, advanced dementia, or brain injury sufficiently severe that it eliminates my abilities to reason and communicate.

Specific Directives for Medical Care

Reversible Illness

In the event of potentially reversible life-threatening illness, I wish to be a FULL CODE and to receive all interventions to save my life, *as long as recovery is possible*, with the ultimate aim of returning home and seeking the goals listed above. Such measures include but are not limited to:

- endotracheal intubation
- mechanical ventilation
- cardiopulmonary resuscitation
- electrical defibrillation
- dialysis
- artificially administered nutrition

Limitations to Care

I consent to the above measures presuming they will enable my recovery from critical illness.

With regard to nonrecoverable illness, or partially recoverable illness with disability, I would accept aggressive measures *if they could help me meet the goals listed above.* In particular, I wish for prolongation of my life if I still possess my mental faculties and can interact meaningfully with others. I would accept long-term ventilator dependence, paralysis, dependence upon others for activities of daily living, and pain if I am still able to converse, write, and reason.

In contrast, I would not accept CPR, endotracheal intubation, mechanical ventilation, or defibrillation in the event of:

1. Nonrecoverable fatal illness.
2. Any illness or disability that permanently impairs my ability to communicate, including but not limited to coma, persistent vegetative state, and minimally conscious state.
3. Advanced dementia.
4. End-stage terminal illness with a life expectancy of six months or less.

I would be unwilling to accept dialysis or artificially administered nutrition for conditions (1) to (3) and would ask for friends, family, and caregivers to instead feed me by hand as I am able to tolerate. However, I *would* accept dialysis and artificially administered nutrition for condition (4), *only* if these measures would grant me more days spent in fellowship, prayer, and reflection, as listed above in my goals.

As a servant of Christ, I seek above all to serve him faithfully. My hope resides in his death and resurrection, for salvation and the forgiveness of sins. "The LORD is my rock and my fortress and my deliverer, my God, my rock, in whom I take refuge" (Ps. 18:2). This side of the cross, I have no fear of death but only joy in his saving work and in the life to come.

APPENDIX 3

Scripture Passages for Comfort

The LORD is my rock and my fortress and my deliverer,
   my God, my rock, in whom I take refuge,
   my shield, and the horn of my salvation, my stronghold.
      (Ps. 18:2)

Even though I walk through the valley of the shadow of
      death,
   I will fear no evil,
for you are with me;
   your rod and your staff,
   they comfort me. (Ps. 23:4)

The LORD is near to the brokenhearted
   and saves the crushed in spirit. (Ps. 34:18)

God is our refuge and strength,
   a very present help in trouble.
Therefore we will not fear though the earth gives way,
   though the mountains be moved into the heart of
      the sea,
though its waters roar and foam,
   though the mountains tremble at its swelling. (Ps. 46:1–3)

But I am like a green olive tree
   in the house of God.

I trust in the steadfast love of God
    forever and ever. (Ps. 52:8)

You guide me with your counsel,
    and afterward you will receive me to glory.
Whom have I in heaven but you?
    And there is nothing on earth that I desire besides you.
My flesh and heart may fail,
    but God is the strength of my heart and my portion
        forever. (Ps. 73:24–26)

I lift up my eyes to the hills.
    From where does my help come?
My help comes from the LORD,
    who made heaven and earth. (Ps. 121:1–2)

Jesus said to her, "I am the resurrection and the life. Whoever believes in me, though he die, yet shall he live, and everyone who lives and believes in me shall never die." (John 11:25–26)

We rejoice in our sufferings, knowing that suffering produces endurance, and endurance produces character, and character produces hope, and hope does not put us to shame, because God's love has been poured into our hearts through the Holy Spirit who has been given to us. (Rom. 5:3–5)

Who shall separate us from the love of Christ? Shall tribulation, or distress, or persecution, or famine, or nakedness, or danger, or sword? As it is written, "For your sake we are being killed all the day long; we are regarded as sheep to be slaughtered." No, in all these things we are more than conquerors through him who loved us. For I am sure that neither death nor life, nor angels nor rulers, nor things present nor things to come, nor powers, nor height nor depth, nor anything else in all creation, will be able to separate us from the love of God in Christ Jesus our Lord. (Rom. 8:35–39)

So we do not lose heart. Thought our outer self is wasting away, our inner self is being renewed day by day. For this light momentary affliction is preparing for us an eternal weight of glory beyond all comparison, as we look not to the things that are seen but to the things that are unseen. For the things that are seen are transient, but the things that are unseen are eternal. (2 Cor. 4:16–18)

But he said to me, "My grace is sufficient for you, for my power is made perfect in weakness." Therefore I will boast all the more gladly of my weaknesses, so that the power of Christ may rest upon me. For the sake of Christ, then, I am content with weaknesses, insults, hardships, persecutions, and calamities. For when I am weak, then I am strong. (2 Cor. 12:9–10)

Blessed be the God and Father of our Lord Jesus Christ! According to his great mercy, he has caused us to be born again to a living hope through the resurrection of Jesus Christ from the dead, to an inheritance that is imperishable, undefiled, and unfading, kept in heaven for you, who by God's power are being guarded through faith for a salvation ready to be revealed in the last time. (1 Pet. 1:3–5)

He will wipe away every tear from their eyes, and death shall be no more, neither shall there be mourning, nor crying, nor pain anymore, for the former things have passed away. And he who was seated on the throne said, "Behold, I am making all things new." (Rev. 21:4–5)

GLOSSARY

acute respiratory distress syndrome (ARDS). A rapidly progressive buildup of fluid in the lungs due to damage of lung capillaries in critical illness.

advance care planning. Discussions and documentation aimed to clarify wishes at the end of life.

advance directive. A document outlining wishes for care at the end of life, with particular emphasis on organ-supporting technologies, and also for designation of a surrogate decision maker.

anaphylaxis. A severe allergic reaction that causes shock and difficulty breathing.

arrhythmia. An abnormal heart rhythm.

arteriovenous (AV) fistula. In dialysis, a surgical connection between an artery and a vein to allow for repeated needle punctures.

aspiration. Inhalation of abnormal contents, usually one's own oral secretions or vomit, into the lungs.

asystole. Complete cessation of electrical activity of the heart.

autonomy. Self-determination; freedom from external control.

bronchial tree. The passageways that transport air from the trachea to the lungs.

capillary. The smallest branch of a blood vessel, carrying blood to and from tissues.

cardiac arrest. When the heart fails to circulate blood flow effectively, due to either abnormal rhythm, inadequate blood volume, poor pump function of the heart, or obstruction to blood flow.

cardiopulmonary resuscitation (CPR). Emergency chest compressions and ventilation to maintain blood flow to the brain when cardiac arrest occurs.

comfort measures only (CMO). A transition in care from treatment aimed toward cure, to treatment that emphasizes palliation of symptoms.

comorbidities. Preexisting chronic diseases.

computed tomography (CT) scan. A diagnostic imaging test that creates detailed cross-sectional images of tissue and internal organs.

continuous venovenous hemofiltration (CVVH). Continuous dialysis, a temporary option for patients who cannot tolerate hemodialysis.

debridement. Removal of damaged or infected tissue from a wound, either with medications, gauze dressings, or surgically with a scalpel or cautery.

delirium. Acute confusion that waxes and wanes, often accompanied by delusions, paranoia, and hallucinations.

dementia. Progressive loss of memory and daily independent functioning, as with Alzheimer's disease.

deoxygenated. Depletion of oxygen.

dialysis. Removal of waste products and excess water from the blood stream as substitute for normal kidney function.

diuretic. Medication that promotes removal of excess water and salt from the body through increased urine production.

electrical cardioversion. An electrical shock administered to the chest to convert an abnormal rhythm back to a regular heartbeat.

electrical defibrillation. An electrical shock administered to the chest to treat cardiac arrest from an abnormal ventricular rhythm; higher voltage than cardioversion.

electrolytes. Minerals with an electric charge (e.g., calcium, magnesium, potassium, sodium) that play a vital role in functions throughout the body.

encephalopathy. A disorder in which a disease or a toxin impairs brain function.

endotracheal tube. A silicone tube placed into the windpipe for mechanical ventilation.

enteral nutrition. Any method of feeding that uses the gastrointestinal tract to deliver a source of calories.

epinephrine. Another term for adrenaline, a hormone that increases blood pressure and quickens heartbeat.

extubation. Removal of an endotracheal tube.

functional status. An individual's ability to perform daily routines necessary to meet basic needs and maintain health.

gastrostomy tube. A surgically placed tube that directly enters the stomach through the abdominal wall.

goals-of-care meeting. A meeting between physicians and a patient or his/her family to determine the next step in care, usually for complex circumstances in the ICU.

healthcare proxy. A document that legally appoints an individual to make healthcare decisions on behalf of a patient in the event that the patient is incapacitated.

hemodialysis. Process of removing waste and fluid and restoring normal electrolyte balance in patients with kidney failure.

hospice. A philosophy of care that focuses on palliation of symptoms at the end of life, with emphasis on quality of life and spiritual and physical well-being.

hypoxia. Low oxygen levels in the bloodstream or body tissues.

iatrogenic. A type of event or complication that occurs secondary to medical interventions.

inotrope. Medication that enhances the ability of the heart to pump. Examples include milrinone, dobutamine, dopamine, and epinephrine (which is also a vasopressor).

intensive care unit (ICU). The department in a hospital where the most seriously ill patients are constantly observed.

intravenous. Medications administered through the bloodstream via access in a vein.

living will. A document completed by a patient, attested to by witnesses, that outlines wishes for end-of-life care.

mechanical ventilator. A machine that provides breathing support.

myocardial infarction. Medical term for heart attack; death of a portion of the heart muscle due to inadequate blood flow.

nasogastric tube. A tube threaded through the nostrils and into the stomach to administer nutrition or remove intestinal contents.

nephrologist. A doctor who specializes in kidney function and disease.

noninvasive positive pressure ventilation (NIPPV). Mechanical ventilation delivered through a facemask or nasal mask rather than through an endotracheal tube.

palliative care. An approach to medical care that focuses on improvement in quality of life at all stages of illness.

perfusion. A supply of oxygen-rich blood.

peritoneum. A membrane lining the abdominal cavity.

pharynx. Medical term for throat.

physician-assisted suicide (PAS). The process of intentionally taking one's life after ingestion of a physician-prescribed lethal dose of medication.

physician orders for life-sustaining treatment (POLST). Legal orders from a physician, formulated in conjunction with a patient, to withhold or administer life-sustaining measures including CPR and mechanical ventilation.

platelets. Cell fragments that circulate throughout the bloodstream and play an essential role in normal blood clotting.

pleural effusion. Fluid in the chest cavity, in the space surrounding the lungs.

pneumonia. Infection of the lungs.

pneumothorax. Accumulation of air in the space between the lung and the chest wall, leading to lung collapse.

post-traumatic stress disorder. A psychiatric disorder that arises in response to a traumatic event and is characterized by nightmares, flashbacks, anxiety, and intrusive thoughts about the event.

pulmonary edema. Fluid within the lung tissue.

pulmonary embolism. When a blood clot becomes lodged in the vessels that carry blood from the heart to the lungs.

pulseless electrical activity (PEA). Cardiac arrest in which the heart continues to beat with a normal electrical rhythm, but disease or injury prevents effective circulation of blood.

renal. Pertaining to the kidneys.

resident. A doctor who has completed medical school but has not yet finished on-the-job training in a specific medical specialty.

respiratory. Pertaining to breathing.

sepsis. A widespread response to infection that reduces blood flow to organs and threatens life.

shock. A condition characterized by inadequate blood flow to organs, resulting in poor oxygen delivery and death if untreated.

solute. One substance dissolved in another.

somnolence. Pathological sleepiness or drowsiness; in medicine it often points to impaired blood flow to the brain or disturbances in breathing.

total parenteral nutrition (TPN). Intravenous feeding, i.e., nutrition administered through the bloodstream, bypassing the gastrointestinal tract.

trachea. Medical term for windpipe.

tracheostomy. Surgical placement of a tube through the neck and into the windpipe to permit connection to a mechanical ventilator.

vasomotor tone. Constriction of blood vessels to maintain blood pressure.

vasopressors. Medications that act on blood vessels to constrict them and elevate blood pressure. Examples include norepinephrine (Levophed), vasopressin, phenylephrine (Neosynephrine), and epinephrine (also an inotrope).

vegetative state. State of unconsciousness and minimal responsiveness, usually from brain injury.

ventilation. Air exchange in breathing, specifically removal of carbon dioxide from the bloodstream.

ventricular fibrillation. An abnormal heart rhythm, leading to cardiac arrest, in which the ventricles contract erratically and fail to pump.

ventricular tachycardia. An abnormal heart rhythm in which the ventricles contract at a rate too high to allow filling with blood; in many cases, this arrhythmia causes cardiac arrest.

voluntary active euthanasia. Deliberate shortening of a patient's life, usually by a physician, through administration of a lethal dose of medication.

NOTES

Chapter 1: Framing the Issue

1. Patients often suspend orders that limit life-sustaining treatment when they undergo surgery, as reversible life-threatening events can arise perioperatively.

2. Dylan Thomas, "Do Not Go Gentle into That Good Night," from *In Country Sleep, and Other Poems* (New York: New Directions, 1952), Academy of American Poets website, accessed August 16, 2018, https.// www.poets.org/poetsorg/poem/do-not-go-gentle-good-night.

3. William Shakespeare, *Hamlet* (Hertfordshire, UK: Wordsworth Editions Ltd., 1992), 60.

4. Robert V. Wells, *Facing the "King of Terrors": Death and Society in an American Community, 1750–1990* (New York: Cambridge University Press, 2000), 195.

5. Liz Hamel, Bryan Wu, and Mollyann Brodie, "Views and Experiences with End-of-Life Medical Care in the U.S.," *The Henry J. Kaiser Family Foundation* (April 2017), accessed January 4, 2018, http://files.kff.org /attachment/Report-Views-and-Experiences-with-End-of-Life-Medical -Care-in-the-US.

6. William Colby, "How We Die in America," an excerpt of *Unplugged: Reclaiming Our Right to Die in America* (New York: Amacom Books, 2006), in AuthorViews.com, accessed January 4, 2018, www.author views.com/authors/Colby/obd.htm.

7. Centers for Disease Control and Prevention National Center for Health Statistics, "Health, United States, 2010: With Special Feature on Death and Dying," accessed January 4, 2018, https://www.cdc.gov/nchs/data /hus/hus10.pdf. See also The Dartmouth Institute for Health Policy and Clinical Practice, "Percent of Deaths Associated with ICU Admission, 2014," *The Dartmouth Atlas of Health Care*, http://www.dartmouthatlas .org/data/table.aspx?ind=14.

8. Rachelle E. Bernacki and Susan D. Block, "Communication about Serious Illness Care Goals: A Review and Synthesis of Best Practices," *JAMA Internal Medicine* 174, no. 12 (2014): 1994–2003.

9. Jaya K. Rao, Lynda A. Anderson, et al., "Completion of Advance Directives Among U.S. Consumers," *American Journal of Preventative Medicine* 46, no. 1 (2014): 65–70.

10. Marta Spranzi and Veronique Fournier, "The Near-Failure of Advance Directives: Why They Should Not Be Abandoned Altogether, But Their Role Radically Reconsidered," *Medicine, Health Care, and Philosophy* 19, no. 4 (2016): 563–64.

11. Zara Cooper, Andrew Courtwright, et al., "Pitfalls in Communication That Lead to Nonbeneficial Surgery in Elderly Patients with Serious Illness: Description of the Problem and Elements of a Solution," *Annals of Surgery* 260, no. 6 (2014): 949–57.

12. Ibid., 949.

13. Natalie C. Ernecoff, Farr A. Curlin, et al., "Healthcare Professionals' Responses to Religious or Spiritual Statements by Surrogate Decision Makers During Goals-of-Care Discussions," *JAMA Internal Medicine* 175, no. 10 (2015): 1662–69.

14. Michael J. Balboni, Adam Sullivan, et al., "Nurse and Physician Barriers to Spiritual Care Provision at the End of Life," *Journal of Pain and Symptom Management* 48, no. 3 (2014): 400–410.

15. Ibid.

16. Tracy A. Balboni, Michael Balboni, et al., "Provision of Spiritual Support to Patients with Advanced Cancer by Religious Communities and Associations with Medical Care at the End of Life," *JAMA Internal Medicine* 173, no. 12 (2013): 1109–17.

Chapter 2: Wisdom Begins with the Word

1. A condensed version of the content in this chapter first appeared online in *Christianity Today*. Kathryn Butler, "When Prolonging Life Means Prolonging Suffering," *Christianity Today* (September 8, 2016), http://www.christianitytoday.com/ct/2016/june-web-only/when-prolonging-life-means-prolonging-suffering.html. Used with permission.

2. Tracy A. Balboni, Michael Balboni, et al., "Provision of Spiritual Support to Patients with Advanced Cancer by Religious Communities and Associations with Medical Care at the End of Life," *JAMA Internal Medicine* 173, no. 12 (2013): 1109–17. See also Andrea C. Phelps, Paul K. Maciejewski, et al., "Religious Coping and Use of Intensive Life-Prolonging Care Near Death in Patients with Advanced Cancer," *Journal of the American Medical Association* 301, no. 11 (2009): 1140–47; Paul K. Maciejewski, Andrea C. Phelps, et al., "Religious Coping and Behavioral Disengagement: Opposing Influences on Advance Care Planning and Receipt of Intensive Care Near Death," *Psycho-Oncology* 21, no. 7 (2012): 714–23.

3. Ann M. Parker, Thiti Sricharoenchai, et al., "Posttraumatic Stress Disorder in Critical Illness Survivors: A Metaanalysis," *Critical Care Medicine* 43, no. 5 (2015): 1121–29.

4. Eduard Kralj, Matej Podbregar, et al., "Frequency and Number of Resuscitation Related Rib and Sternum Fractures Are Higher Than Generally Considered," *Resuscitation* 93 (2015): 136–41.

Chapter 3: Resuscitation for Cardiac Arrest

1. Dylan Harris and Hannah Willoughby, "Resuscitation on Television: Realistic or Ridiculous? A Quantitative Observational Analysis of the Portrayal of Cardiopulmonary Resuscitation in Television Medical Drama," *Resuscitation* 80, no. 11 (2009): 1275–79. See also Jochen Hinkelbein, Oliver Spelten, et al., "An Assessment of Resuscitation Quality in the Television Drama Emergency Room: Guideline Non-Compliance and Low-Quality Cardiopulmonary Resuscitation Lead to a Favorable Outcome?," *Resuscitation* 85, no. 8 (2014): 1106–10; Jaclyn Portanova, Krystle Irvine, et al., "It Isn't Like This on TV: Revisiting CPR Survival Rates Depicted on Popular TV Shows," *Resuscitation* 96 (2015): 148–50.

2. Portanova, Irvine, et al., "*It Isn't Like This on TV*," 148–50.

3. Ibid.

4. Derrick H. Adams and David P. Snedden, "How Misconceptions among Elderly Patients Regarding Survival Outcomes of Inpatient Cardiopulmonary Resuscitation Affect Do-Not-Resuscitate Orders," *The Journal of the American Osteopathic Association* 106 (2006): 402–4.

5. Ibid., 402.

6. Guillermo Gutierrez, "Cellular Effects of Hypoxemia and Ischemia," in *The Lung: Scientific Foundations*, 2nd ed., ed. Ronald G. Crystal et al. (Philadelphia: Lippincott-Raven, 1997), 1969. See also Thomas F. Hornbein, "Hypoxia and the Brain," in *The Lung: Scientific Foundations*, 1981.

7. Thomas D. Rea, Mickey S. Eisenberg, et al., "Temporal Trends in Sudden Cardiac Arrest: A 25-Year Emergency Medical Services Perspective," *Circulation* 107, no. 22 (2003): 2780–85.

8. Mads Wissenberg, Freddy K. Lippert, et al., "Association of National Initiatives to Improve Cardiac Arrest Management with Rates of Bystander Intervention and Patient Survival Out-of-Hospital Cardiac Arrest," *Journal of the American Medical Association* 310, no. 13 (2013): 1377–84.

9. Peter G. Brindley, Darren M. Markland, et al., "Predictors of Survival Following In-Hospital Adult Cardiopulmonary Resuscitation," *Canadian Medical Association Journal* 167, no. 4 (2002): 343–48. See also Heather L. Bloom, Irfan Shukrullah, et al., "Long-Term Survival After Successful Inhospital Cardiac Arrest Resuscitation," *American Heart Journal* 153, no. 5 (2007): 831–36; Zachary D. Goldberger, Paul S. Chan,

et al., "Duration of Resuscitation Efforts and Survival after In-Hospital Cardiac Arrest: An Observational Study," *The Lancet* 380, no. 9852 (2012): 1473–81; Paul S. Chan, Bryan McNally, et al., "Recent Trends in Survival from Out-of-Hospital Cardiac Arrest in the United States," *Circulation* 130, no. 21 (2014): 1876–78; Michael K. Y. Wong, Laurie J. Morrison, et al., "Trends in Short- and Long-Term Survival among Out-of-Hospital Cardiac Arrest Patients Alive at Hospital Arrival," *Circulation* 130, no. 21 (2014): 1883–90.

10. C. R. Green, J. A. Botha, and R. Tiruvoipati, "Cognitive Function, Quality of Life and Mental Health in Survivors of Out-of-Hospital Cardiac Arrest: A Review," *Anaesthesia and Intensive Care* 43, no. 5 (2015): 569.

11. Eduard Kralj, Matej Podbregar, et al., "Frequency and Number of Resuscitation Related Rib and Sternum Fractures Are Higher Than Generally Considered," *Resuscitation* 93 (2015): 136–41.

12. J. J. De Vreede-Swagemakers, A. P. Gorgels, et al., "Circumstances and Causes of Out-of-Hospital Cardiac Arrest in Sudden Death Survivors," *Heart* 79, no. 4 (1998): 356–61.

13. Ibid. See also Sidney Goldstein, Richard Landis, et al., "Characteristics of the Resuscitated Out-of-Hospital Cardiac Arrest Victim with Coronary Artery Disease," *Circulation* 64, no. 5 (1981): 977–84; Rea et al., "Temporal Trends," 2780–85; Jared T. Bunch, Roger White, et al., "Outcomes and In-Hospital Treatment of Out-of-Hospital Cardiac Arrest Patients Resuscitated from Ventricular Fibrillation by Early Defibrillation," *Mayo Clinic Proceedings* 79, no. 5 (2004): 613–19.

14. De Vreede-Swagemakers et al., "Causes of Out-of-Hospital Cardiac Arrest," 356–61. See also Goldstein et al., "Cardiac Arrest Victim with Coronary Artery Disease," 977–84; Rea et al., "Temporal Trends," 2780–85; Bunch et al., "Outcomes Ventricular Fibrillation," 613–19.

15. Rea et al., "Temporal Trends," 2780–85. See also M. Kuisma and A. Alaspää, "Out-of-Hospital Cardiac Arrests of Non-Cardiac Origin; Epidemiology and Outcome," *European Heart Journal* 18, no. 7 (1997): 1122–28; Johan Engdahl, Angela Bång, et al., "Can We Define Patients with No and Those with Some Chance of Survival When Found in Asystole Out of Hospital?" *American Journal of Cardiology* 86, no. 6 (2000): 610–14; William A. Gray, Robert J. Capone, and Albert S. Most, "Unsuccessful Emergency Medical Resuscitation: Are Continued Efforts in the Emergency Department Justified?" *New England Journal of Medicine* 325, no. 20 (1991): 1393–98; Robert L. Levine, Marvin A. Wayne, and Charles C. Miller, "End-Tidal Carbon Dioxide and Outcome of Out-of-Hospital Cardiac Arrest," *New England Journal of Medicine* 337, no. 5 (1997): 301–6.

16. De Vreede-Swagemakers et al., "Causes of Out-of-Hospital Cardiac Arrest," 356–61; H. Leon Greene, "Sudden Arrhythmic Cardiac Death: Mechanisms—Resuscitation and Classification: The Seattle Perspective," *American Journal of Cardiology* 65, no. 4 (1990): 4B–12B;

Thomas H. Marwick, Colin C. Case, et al., "Prediction of Survival from Resuscitation: A Prognostic Index Derived from Multivariate Logistic Model Analysis," *Resuscitation* 22, no. 2 (1991): 129–37.

Chapter 4: Introduction to Intensive Care

1. Portions of this chapter first appeared in my "Christian, Your Pain Is Never Punishment," Desiring God website (February 2, 2017), https://www.desiringgod.org/articles/christian-your-pain-is-never-punishment. Used with permission.
2. Jack E. Zimmerman, Andrew A. Kramer, and William A. Knaus, "Changes in Hospital Mortality for United States Intensive Care Unit Admissions from 1988 to 2012," *Critical Care* 17, no. 2 (2013): 1–9.
3. Ibid.
4. Gerald L. Weinhouse, "Delirium and Sleep Disturbances in the Intensive Care Unit: Can We Do Better?" *Current Opinion in Anaesthesiology* 27, no. 4 (2014): 403.
5. Alexi A. Wright, Nancy L. Keating, et al., "Place of Death: Correlations with Quality of Life of Patients with Cancer and Predictors of Bereaved Caregivers' Mental Health," *Journal of Clinical Oncology* 28, no. 29 (2010): 4457–64.
6. James C. Jackson, Pratik P. Pandharipande, et al., "Depression, Post-Traumatic Stress Disorder, and Functional Disability in Survivors of Critical Illness in the BRAIN-ICU Study: A Longitudinal Cohort Study," *The Lancet Respiratory Medicine* 2, no. 5 (2014): 369–79.
7. Ann M. Parker, Thiti Sricharoenchai, et al., "Posttraumatic Stress Disorder in Critical Illness Survivors: A Metaanalysis," *Critical Care Medicine* 43, no. 5 (2015): 1121–29.
8. Charles S. Milliken, Jennifer L. Auchterlonie, and Charles W. Hoge, "Longitudinal Assessment of Mental Health Problems Among Active and Reserve Component Soldiers Returning from the Iraq War," *Journal of the American Medical Association* 298, no. 18 (2007): 2141–49.
9. Scott K. Fridkin, Sharon F. Welbel, and Robert A. Weinstein, "Magnitude and Prevention of Nosocomial Infections in the Intensive Care Unit," *Infectious Disease Clinics of North America* 11, no. 2 (1997): 479–96.
10. Jean-Louis Vincent, Jordi Rello, et al., "International Study of the Prevalence and Outcomes of Infection in Intensive Care Units," *Journal of the American Medical Association* 302, no. 21 (2009): 2323–29.
11. Greet Hermans, Bernard De Jonghe, et al., "Clinical Review: Critical Illness Polyneuropathy and Myopathy," *Critical Care* 12, no. 6 (2008): 238–47.
12. Jeremy Kahn, Derek C. Angus, et al., "The Epidemiology of Chronic Critical Illness in the United States," *Critical Care Medicine* 43, no. 2 (2015): 284–85.
13. Frédéric Pochard, Eli Azoulay, et al., "Symptoms of Anxiety and Depression in Family Members of Intensive Care Unit Patients: Ethical

Hypothesis Regarding Decision-Making Capacity," *Critical Care Medicine* 29, no. 10 (2001): 1893–97; Eli Azoulay, Frédéric Pochard, et al., "Risk of Post-Traumatic Stress Symptoms in Family Members of Intensive Care Unit Patients," *American Journal of Respiratory and Critical Care Medicine* 171, no. 9 (2005): 987–94; Mark D. Siegel, Earle Hayes, et al., "Psychiatric Illness in the Next of Kin of Patients Who Die in the Intensive Care Unit," *Critical Care Medicine* 36, no. 6 (2008): 1722–28.

Chapter 5: Mechanical Ventilation

1. Jaya K. Rao, Lynda A. Anderson, Feng-Chang Lin, and Jeffrey P. Laux, "Completion of Advance Directives Among U.S. Consumers," *American Journal of Preventative Medicine* 46, no 1 (2014): 65–70.

2. Selected content from this chapter was adapted from my article "The Breath of Life," Desiring God website, December 14, 2016, https://www.desiringgod.org/articles/the-breath-of-life. Used with permission.

3. Armando Rotondi, Lakshmipathi Chelluri, et al., "Patients' Recollections of Stressful Experiences While Receiving Prolonged Mechanical Ventilation in an Intensive Care Unit," *Critical Care Medicine* 30, no. 4 (2002): 746–52.

4. Ibid.

5. Ibid. See also Jill L. Guttormson, Karin Lindstrom Bremer, and Rachel M. Jones, "'Not Being Able to Talk Was Horrid': A Descriptive, Correlational Study of Communication During Mechanical Ventilation," *Intensive and Critical Care Nursing* 31 (2015): 180.

6. Ibid., 179–86.

7. Michael Klompas, Richard Branson, et al., "Strategies to Prevent Ventilator-Associated Pneumonia in Acute Care Hospitals: 2014 Update," *Infection Control and Hospital Epidemiology* 35, no. 8 (2014): 915–36.

8. C. G. Adair, S. P. Gorman, et al., "Implications of Endotracheal Tube Biofilm for Ventilator-Associated Pneumonia," *Intensive Care Medicine* 25, no. 10 (1999): 1072–76.

9. Jean-Marc Tadié, Eva Behm, et al., "Post-Intubation Laryngeal Injuries and Extubation Failure: A Fiberoptic Endoscopic Study," *Intensive Care Medicine* 36, no. 6 (2010): 991–98.

10. American Thoracic Society, European Respiratory Society, et al., "International Consensus Conference in Intensive Care Medicine: Noninvasive Positive Pressure Ventilation in Acute Respiratory Failure," *American Journal of Respiratory and Critical Care Medicine* 163, no. 1 (2001): 283–91.

11. Miquel Ferrer and Antoni Torres, "Noninvasive Ventilation for Acute Respiratory Failure," *Current Opinion in Critical Care* 21, no. 1 (2015): 1–6.

12. Alexandre Demoule, Emmanuelle Girou, et al., "Benefits and Risks of Success or Failure of Noninvasive Ventilation," *Intensive Care Medicine* 32, no. 11 (2006): 1756–65.

Chapter 6: Cardiovascular Support

1. Katie Scales, "Arterial Catheters: Indications, Insertion, and Use in Critical Care," *British Journal of Nursing* 19 (2010): S16–S21.
2. Ibid.
3. David C. McGee and Michael K. Gould, "Preventing Complications of Central Venous Catheterization," *New England Journal of Medicine* 348, no. 12 (2003): 1123–33; Lewis A. Eisen, Mangala Narasimhan, et al., "Mechanical Complications of Central Venous Catheters," *Journal of Intensive Care Medicine* 21, no. 1 (2006): 40–46.
4. Sheldon A. Magder, "The Highs and Lows of Blood Pressure: Toward Meaningful Clinical Targets in Patients with Shock," *Critical Care Medicine* 42, no. 5 (2014): 1241–51.

Chapter 7: Artificially Administered Nutrition

1. Joshua E. Van de Vathorst Perry, Larry R. Churchill, and Howard S. Kirshner, "The Terri Schiavo Case: Legal, Ethical, and Medical Perspectives," *Annals of Internal Medicine* 143, no. 10 (2005): 744–48.
2. Michael P. Casaer and Greet Van Den Berge, "Nutrition in the Acute Phase of Critical Illness," *New England Journal of Medicine* 370, no. 25 (2014): 1227–36.
3. Casaer et al., "Nutrition," 1227.
4. Stéphane Villet, René L. Chiolero, et al., "Negative Impact of Hypocaloric Feeding and Energy Balance on Clinical Outcomes in ICU Patients," *Clinical Nutrition* 24, no. 4 (2005): 502–9; Lewis Rubinson, Gregory B. Diette, et al., "Low Caloric Intake Is Associated with Nosocomial Bloodstream Infections in Patients in the Medical Intensive Care Unit," *Critical Care Medicine* 32, no. 2 (2004): 350–57. Cathy Alberda, Leah Gramlich, et al., "The Relationship between Nutritional Intake and Clinical Outcomes in Critically Ill Patients: Results of an International Multicenter Observational Study," *Intensive Care Medicine* 35, no. 10 (2009): 1728–37.
5. William N. Baskin, "Acute Complications Associated with Bedside Placement of Feeding Tubes," *Nutrition in Clinical Practice* 21, no. 1 (2006): 40–55.
6. Stephen A. McClave, Mark T. DeMeo, et al., "North American Summit on Aspiration in the Critically Ill Patient: Consensus Statement," *Journal of Parenteral and Enteral Nutrition* 26, suppl. 6 (2002): S80–85.
7. Vivian Christine Luft, Mariur Gomes Beghetto, et al., "Role of Enteral Nutrition in the Incidence of Diarrhea Among Hospitalized Adult Patients," *Nutrition* 24, no. 6 (2008): 528–35; Beth E. Taylor, Stephen A. McClave, et al., "Guidelines for the Provision and Assessment of Nutrition Support Therapy in the Adult Critically Ill Patient: Society for Critical Care Medicine (SCCM) and American Society for Parenteral and Enteral Nutrition (A.S.P.E.N.)," *Critical Care Medicine* 44, no. 2 (2016): 390–438.

8. Claudio A. R. Gomes Jr., Regis B. Andriolo, et al., "Percutaneous Endoscopic Gastrostomy Versus Nasogastric Tube Feeding for Adults with Swallowing Disturbances," *Cochrane Database of Systematic Reviews* 5, article no. CD008096 (2015), 15.
9. Ibid., 16. See also Baskin et al., "Acute Complications," 45.
10. Baskin et al., "Acute Complications," 46.
11. Taylor et al., "Nutrition Support Therapy," 396–97.
12. Ibid., 406–8.
13. Cynthia M. A. Geppert, Maria R. Andrews, and Mary Ellen Druyan, "Ethical Issues in Artificial Nutrition and Hydration: A Review," *Journal of Parenteral and Enteral Nutrition* 34, no. 1 (2010): 79–88; Suzanne van de Vathorst, "Artificial Nutrition at the End of Life: Ethical Issues," *Best Practices and Research, Clinical Gastroenterology* 28, no. 2 (2014): 247–53; Nobuhisa Nakajima, Yoshinobu Hata, and Kenju Kusumuto, "A Clinical Study on the Influence of Hydration Volume on the Signs of Terminally Ill Cancer Patients with Abdominal Malignancies," *Journal of Palliative Medicine* 16, no. 2 (2013): 185–89.
14. Geppert et al., "Ethical Issues in Artificial Nutrition," 83–84; Van de Vathorst, "Artificial Nutrition at the End of Life," 247–49.
15. Nobuhisa et al., "Hydration Volume," 185–89.
16. American Geriatrics Society Ethics Committee and Clinical Practice and Models of Care Committee, "American Geriatrics Society Feeding Tubes in Advanced Dementia Position Statement," *Journal of the American Geriatrics Society* 62, no. 8 (2014): 1590–93; Robert E. Lam and Peter J. Lam, "Nutrition in Dementia," *Canadian Medical Association Journal* 186, no. 17 (2014): 1319.
17. Joan M. Teno, Pedro L. Gozalo, et al., "Does Feeding Tube Insertion and Its Timing Improve Survival?" *Journal of the American Geriatrics Society* 60, no. 10 (2012): 1918–21; Christopher M. Callahan, Kathy M. Haag, et al., "Outcomes of Percutaneous Endoscopic Gastrostomy Among Older Adults in a Community Setting," *Journal of the American Geriatrics Society* 48, no. 9 (2000): 1048–54; Joan M. Teno, Pedro Gozalo, et al., "Feeding Tubes and the Prevention or Healing of Pressure Ulcers," *Archives of Internal Medicine* 172, no. 9 (2012): 697–701.
18. Jane L. Givens, Kevin Selby, et al., "Hospital Transfers of Nursing Home Residents with Dementia," *Journal of the American Geriatrics Society* 60, no. 5 (2012): 905–9.

Chapter 8: Dialysis

1. Paul M. Palevsky, Jane Hongyuan Zhang, et al., "Intensity of Renal Support in Critically Ill Patient with Acute Kidney Injury," *New England Journal of Medicine* 359, no. 1 (2008): 7–20; Danilo Fliser, Maurice Laville, et al., "A European Best Practice (ERBP) Position Statement on the Kidney Disease Improving Global Outcomes (KDIGO) Clincial Practice Guidelines on Acute Kidney Injury, Part 1: Definitions, Conservative

Management and Contrast-Induced Nephropathy," *Nephrology Dialysis Transplantation* 27, no. 12 (2012): 4263–72.

2. Ibid., 7–20.

3. Paula Dennen, Ivor S. Douglas, and Robert Anderson, "Acute Kidney Injury in the Intensive Care Unit: An Update and Primer for the Intensivist," *Critical Care Medicine* 38, no. 1 (2010): 261–75.

4. Allan J. Collins, Robert N. Foley, et al., "Excerpts from the United States Renal Data System 2009 Annual Data Report: Atlas of End-Stage Renal Disease in the United States," *American Journal of Kidney Diseases* 55, suppl. 1 (2010): S1.

5. Pietro Ravani, Suetonia C. Palmer, et al., "Associations Between Hemodialysis Access Type and Clinical Outcomes: A Systematic Review," *Journal of the American Society of Nephrology* 24, no. 3 (2013): 465–73.

6. Stephen D. Weisbord, "Symptoms and Their Correlates in Chronic Kidney Disease," *Advances in Chronic Kidney Disease* 14, no. 4 (2007): 319–27.

7. Ibid.

8. Ibid.

9. Jonathan Himmelfarb and T. Alp Ikizler, "Hemodialysis," *New England Journal of Medicine* 363, no. 19 (2010): 1839; Alvin H. Moss, "Revised Dialysis Clinical Practice Guideline Promotes More Informed Decision-Making," *Clinical Journal of the American Society of Nephrology* 5, no. 12 (2010): 2380.

10. Himmelfarb et al., "Hemodialysis," 1839–40.

11. Moss, "Clinical Practice Guideline," 2380–83.

12. Ibid.

13. Ibid.

14. Daisy J. A. Janssen, Martijn A. Spruit, et al., "Insight into Advance Care Planning for Patients on Dialysis," *Journal of Pain and Symptom Management* 45, no. 1 (2013): 104–13.

15. Manjula Kurella Tamura, Kenneth E. Covinsky, et al., "Functional Status of Elderly Adults Before and After Initiation of Dialysis," *New England Journal of Medicine* 361, no. 16 (2009): 1539–47.

16. Moss, "Clinical Practice Guideline," 2380–83.

Chapter 9: Brain Injury

1. Content from this chapter was adapted from my article "Words We Dread to Hear: Coma, Brain Death, and Christian Hope," Desiring God website, November 21, 2016, https://www.desiringgod.org/articles/words-we-dread-to-hear. Used with permission.

2. James L. Bernat, "The Natural History of Chronic Disorders of Consciousness," *Neurology* 75, no. 3 (2010): 206–7.

3. Ibid., 206.

4. Calixto Machado, Julius Kerein, et al., "The Concept of Brain Death Did Not Evolve to Benefit Organ Transplants," *Journal of Medical Ethics* 33, no. 4 (2007): 197–200.

5. Martin Smith, "Physiologic Changes During Brain Stem Death—Lessons for Management of the Organ Donor," *The Journal of Heart and Lung Transplantation* 23, no. 9 (2004): S217–22.

6. The National Conference of Commissioners on Uniform State Law, "Determination of Death Act Summary," Uniform Law Commission, accessed January 8, 2018, http://www.uniformlaws.org/ActSummary .aspx?title=Determination%20of%20Death%20Act.

7. Quality Standards Subcommittee of the American Academy of Neurology, "Practice Parameters for Determining Brain Death in Adults," *Neurology* 45, no. 5 (1995): 1012–14.

8. Christian Medical and Dental Association House of Representatives, "Death Ethics Statement," Christian Medical and Dental Association (2004), accessed January 8, 2018, https://www.cmda.org/resources /publication/death-ethics-statement.

9. Pope John Paul II, "Address of the Holy Father John Paul II to the Eighteenth International Congress of the Transplantation Society," Vatican, August 29, 2000, accessed January 8, 2018, http://w2 .vatican.va/content/john-paul-ii/en/speeches/2000/jul-sep/documents /hf_jp-ii spe_20000829_transplants.html.

10. Shivani Ghoshal and David M. Greer, "Why Is Diagnosing Brain Death So Confusing?" *Current Opinion in Critical Care* 21, no. 2 (2015): 107–12.

Chapter 10: Comfort Measures and Hospice

1. Matthieu Schmidt and Elie Azoulay, "Having a Loved One in the ICU: The Forgotten Family," *Current Opinion in Critical Care* 18, no. 5 (2012): 540–47.

2. Ziad Obermeyer, Maggie Makar, et al., "Association Between the Medicare Hospice Benefit and Health Care Utilization and Costs for Patients with Poor-Prognosis Cancer," *Journal of the American Medical Association* 312, no. 18 (2014): 1888–96.

3. Stephen R. Connor, Bruce Pyenson, et al., "Comparing Hospice and Non-hospice Patient Survival among Patients Who Die within a Three-Year Window," *Journal of Pain and Symptom Management* 33, no. 3 (2007): 238–46; Akiko M. Saito, Mary Beth Landrum, et al., "Hospice Care and Survival among Elderly Patients with Lung Cancer," *Journal of Palliative Medicine* 14, no. 8 (2011): 929–39.

4. Alexi A. Wright, Nancy L. Keating, et al., "Place of Death: Correlation with Quality of Life in Patients with Cancer and Predictors of Bereaved Caregivers' Mental Health," *Journal of Clinical Oncology* 28, no. 29 (2010): 4457–64.

5. Ibid.

6. Ellen P. McCarthy, Risa B. Burns, et al., "Hospice Use Among Medicare Managed Care and Fee-for-Service Patients Dying with Cancer," *Journal of the American Medical Association* 289, no. 17 (2003): 2238–45.
7. National Hospice and Palliative Care Organization, "Facts and Figures: Hospice Care in America," 2016 ed. (October 2017), https://www.nhpco.org/sites/default/files/public/Statistics_Research/2016_Facts_Figures.pdf.
8. Erica R. Schockett, Joan M. Teno, et al., "Late Referral to Hospice and Bereaved Family Member Perception of Quality of End-of-Life Care," *Journal of Pain and Symptom Management* 30, no. 5 (2003): 400–407; Pallavi Kumar, Alexi A. Wright, et al., "Family Perspectives on Hospice Care Experiences of Patients with Cancer," *Journal of Clinical Oncology* 35, no. 4 (2017): 432–39.
9. Liz Hamel, Bryan Wu, and Mollyann Brodie, "Views and Experiences with End-of-Life Medical Care in the U.S.," *The Henry J. Kaiser Family Foundation* (April 2017), accessed January 4, 2018, http://files.kff.org/attachment
10. Paula Lusardi, Paul Jodka, et al., "The Going Home Initiative: Getting Critical Care Patients Home with Hospice," *Critical Care Nurse* 31, no. 5 (2011): 46.
11. Thomas W. DeCato, Ruth A. Engelberg, et al., "Hospital Variation and Temporal Trends in Palliative Care and End-of-Life Care in the ICU," *Critical Care Medicine* 14, no. 6 (2013): 1405–11.
12. Leslie P. Scheunemann, Michelle McDevitt, et al., "Randomized, Controlled Trials of Interventions to Improve Communication in Intensive Care: A Systematic Review," *Chest* 139, no. 3 (2011): 543–54; Ciarán T. Bradley and Karen J. Brasel, "Developing Guidelines That Identify Patients Who Would Benefit from Palliative Care Services in the Surgical Intensive Care Unit," *Critical Care Medicine* 37, no. 3 (2009): 946–50.
13. Craig D. Blinderman and J. Andrew Billings, "Comfort Care for Patients Dying in the Hospital," *New England Journal of Medicine* 373, no. 26 (2015): 2549–61.

Chapter 11: The Dangers of Physician-Assisted Suicide

1. United States Census Bureau, Population Division, "Annual Estimates of the Resident Population for the United States: Regions, States, and Puerto Rico: April 1, 2010 to July 1, 2016," United States Census Bureau (December 2016), accessed January 8, 2018, https://www2.census.gov/programs-surveys/popest/tables/2010-2016/state/totals/nst-est2016-01.xlsx.
2. Oregon Health Authority Public Health Division, Center for Health Statistics, "Oregon Death with Dignity Act: Data Summary 2016," Oregon.gov (February 10, 2017), accessed January 8, 2018, http://www.oregon.gov/oha/ph/providerpartnerresources/evaluationresearch/deathwithdignityact/Documents/year19.pdf.
3. Dr. Jack Kevorkian was an American pathologist who staunchly advocated for euthanasia in the 1980s and 1990s. He personally assisted in

the deaths of over one hundred people, and in 1999 was convicted of second-degree murder for administering a lethal injection to a patient with amytrophic lateral sclerosis.

4. Compassion and Choices, "About Compassion and Choices" (2016), accessed January 8, 2018, https://www.compassionandchoices.org/wp-content/up loads/2016/02/About-Compassion-and-Choices-Brochure-FINAL-4.05 .16-Approved-for-Public-Distribution.pdf.

5. Ezekiel J. Emanuel, Bregje D. Onwuteaka-Philipsen, et al., "Attitudes and Practices of Euthanasia and Physician-Assisted Suicide in the United States," *Journal of the American Medical Association* 316, no. 1 (2016): 79–90.

6. American Medical Association, "Chapter 5: Opinions on Caring for Patients at the End of Life," American Medical Association Principles of Ethics (2016), accessed January 8, 2018, https://www.ama-assn.org/sites /default/files/media-browser/code-of-medical-ethics-chapter-5.pdf.

7. Ewan C. Goligher, E. Wesley Ely, et al., "Physician-Assisted Suicide and Euthanasia in the ICU: A Dialogue on Core Ethical Issues," *Critical Care Medicine* 46, no. 2 (2017): 149–55.

8. Emaniel et al., "Euthanasia and Physician-Assisted Suicide," 81.

9. Ibid.

10. Charles Blanke, Michael LeBlanc, and Dawn Hershman, "Characterizing Eighteen Years of the Death with Dignity Act in Oregon," *Journal of the American Medical Association Oncology* 3, no. 10 (2017): 1403–6.

11. Ibid.

12. Lois A. Bowers, "Atul Gawande: Senior Living Vital to Person-Centered Care," McKnight's Senior Living (June 23, 2016), accessed January 8, 2018, http://www.mcknightsseniorliving.com /news/atul-gawande-senior-living-vital-to-person-centered-care/article /505342/.

Chapter 12: Advance Care Planning

1. Maria J. Silveira, Scott Y. H. Kim, and Kenneth M. Langa, "Advance Directives and Outcomes of Surrogate Decision Making Before Death," *New England Journal of Medicine* 362, no. 13 (2010): 1211–18.

2. Ibid. See also Karen M. Detering, Andrew D. Hancock, et al., "The Impact of Advance Care Planning on End of Life Care in Elderly Patients: Randomised Controlled Trial," *British Medical Journal* 34, no. c1345 (2010): 1–9; Alexi A. Wright, Baohui Zhang, et al., "Associations Between End-of-Life Discussions, Patient Mental Health, Medical Care Near Death, and Caregiver Bereavement Adjustment," *Journal of the American Medical Association* 300, no. 14 (2008): 1665–73.

3. Detering et al., "The Impact of Advance Care Planning," 1–9.

4. Yan S. Kim, Gabriel J. Escobar, et al., "The Natural History of Changes in Preferences for Life-Sustaining Treatments and Implications for Inpatient

Mortality in Younger and Older Hospitalized Patients," *Journal of the American Geriatrics Society* 64, no. 5 (2016): 981–89.

5. David Wendler and Annette Rid, "Systematic Review: The Effect on Surrogates of Making Treatment Decisions for Others," *Annals of Internal Medicine* 154, no. 5 (2011): 336–46.

6. Melissa A. Z. Marks and Hal R. Arkes, "Patient and Surrogate Disagreement in End-of-Life Decisions: Can Surrogates Accurately Predict Patients' Preferences?" *Medical Decision Making* 28, no. 4 (2008): 524–31; David I. Shalowitz, Elizabeth Garrett-Mayer, and David Wendler, "The Accuracy of Surrogate Decision Makers: A Systematic Review," *Archives of Internal Medicine* 166, no. 5 (2006): 493–97.

7. Ursula K. Braun, "Experiences with POLST: Opportunities for Improving Advance Care Planning," *Journal of General Internal Medicine* 31, no. 10 (2016): 1111–12; Susan E. Hickman, Elisabeth Keevern, and Bernard J. Hammes, "Use of the Physician Orders for Life-Sustaining Treatment Program in the Clinical Setting: A Systematic Review of the Literature," *Journal of the American Geriatrics Society* 63, no. 2 (2015): 341–50.

8. Braun, "Experiences with POLST," 1111–12; Hickman et al., "Use of Physician Orders," 341–50.

Chapter 13: Being a Voice

1. Maria J. Silveira, Scott Y. H. Kim, and Kenneth M. Langa, "Advance Directives and Outcomes of Surrogate Decision Making Before Death," *New England Journal of Medicine* 362, no. 13 (2010): 1211–18.

2. Elizabeth K. Vig, Helene Starks, et al., *Journal of General Internal Medicine* 22, no. 9 (2007): 1274–79.

3. David Wendler and Annette Rid, "Systematic Review: The Effect on Surrogates of Making Treatment Decisions for Others," *Annals of Internal Medicine* 154, no. 5 (2011): 336–46.

4. David I. Shalowitz, Elizabeth Garrett-Mayer, and David Wendler, "The Accuracy of Surrogate Decision Makers: A Systematic Review," *Archives of Internal Medicine* 166, no. 5 (2006): 493–97.

5. Danielle R. Probst, Jillian L. Gustin, et al., "ICU versus Non-ICU Hospital Death: Family Member Complicated Grief, Posttraumatic Stress, and Depressive Symptoms," *Journal of Palliative Medicine* 19, no. 4 (2016): 387–93; Mark D. Siegel, Earle Hayes, et al., "Psychiatric Illness in the Next of Kin of Patients Who Die in the Intensive Care Unit," *Critical Care Medicine* 36, no. 6 (2008): 1722–28.

FURTHER READING

Books

Card, Michael. *A Sacred Sorrow: Reaching Out to God in the Lost Language of Lament*. Colorado Springs, CO: NavPress, 2005.
A beautifully-written and theologically rich exploration of biblical expressions of lament, with extrapolations to modern struggles with grief.

Dunlop, John, MD. *Finishing Well to the Glory of God: Strategies from a Christian Physician*. Wheaton, IL: Crossway, 2011.
Dr. Dunlop offers believers a beautiful, tenderly written guide to resting in the arms of Christ at the end of life. He weaves medical advice throughout a narrative that at some points reads like a memoir and at other times like a devotional.

Gawande, Atul. *Being Mortal: Medicine and What Matters in the End*. Reprint ed. New York: Picador, 2017.
Although he does not write from a Christian perspective, Dr. Gawande offers invaluable insight to aging, nursing-home care, hospice, and care goals in his best-selling book.

Jacobs, Martha R. *A Clergy Guide to End-of-Life Issues*. Cleveland, OH: Pilgrim Press, 2010.
An accessible, clearly written, and practical guide to end-of-life care, with clergy as a target audience.

Moll, Rob. *The Art of Dying: Living Fully in the Life to Come*. Downers Grove, IL: InterVarsity Press, 2010.
Christianity Today editor Rob Moll offers a candid survey of how medical advancements have changed our experience of death, and explores how to face life's end with our eyes on the cross.

Orr, R. *Medical Ethics and the Faith Factor: A Handbook for Clergy and Health-Care Professionals*. Grand Rapids, MI: Eerdmans, 2009.
Comprehensive, thorough, thoughtful; an excellent resource in medical bioethics, with attention to Christian theology.

Van Drunen, David. *Bioethics and the Christian Life: A Guide to Making Difficult Decisions*. Wheaton, IL: Crossway, 2009.
A survey of multiple issues in bioethics, this thoughtful book includes a chapter on end-of-life care, with an emphasis on broad principles.

Websites

Christian Medical and Dental Association (CMDA), https://www.cmda.org.
A site geared toward medical and dental professionals who follow Christ. The "Issues and Ethics" page includes helpful statements on various ethical dilemmas, with an emphasis on the Bible.

Christian Medical Fellowship, http://www.cmf.org.uk/advocacy/end-of-life/.
The UK correlate to the CMDA. A site geared toward Christian medical professionals; however, the end-of-life page includes helpful links and resources for laypeople.

Five Wishes Program, https://www.agingwithdignity.org/five-wishes/about-five-wishes.
A program that guides individuals through drafting a living will. Offers helpful prompts and has clear, understandable language.

GriefShare, https://www.griefshare.org.
A Christian support group for people grieving the death of a family member or loved one, with thousands of meetings occurring weekly worldwide.

National Hospice and Palliative Care Organization, https://www.caringinfo.org.
Includes information on hospice and palliative care, as well as a repository of downloadable advance directive forms from all states in the US.

National POLST Paradigm, http://www.POLST.org.
An online repository of orders for life-sustaining treatment from every state.

GENERAL INDEX

acute respiratory distress syndrome (ARDS), 77–78, 193
advance care planning: advance directives, 17, 24, 26, 70, 97, 134, 149–69, 185–88, 193, 214; healthcare proxies, 26, 149, 153–54, 164, 168, 185, 195; living wills, 149–64, 185, 195, 214; surrogate decision making, 28, 149–64, 165–74, 185, 193
aggressive treatments: may cause suffering, 15, 29, 32, 34, 38, 41–43, 67, 122, 183; may prolong dying, 58, 63, 77–80, 96–97, 101, 109, 118, 130, 151, 160, 169, 173–75, 185
Alzheimer's disease, 56, 97, 194
American Academy of Neurology, 119, 208n7
American Geriatrics Society, 97
American Medical Association, 141–42
antibiotics, 60, 62, 64, 94
anxiety: of family members, 42, 66–67, 129, 151, 164, 172–74, 196; of patients, 23, 41–42, 67, 75, 127, 132–37, 196
arrhythmia, 53, 88, 181, 193, 197
arterial lines (A-lines), 85–88, 183
artificially administered nutrition: advance directives for, 89–90, 98, 118, 163, 187–88; overview

of, 89–100; potential harm of, 25, 90, 92–99, 183
autonomy, 31–32, 141–47, 157–58, 168, 177, 193

Being Mortal, 145, 213
Bible, the: suffering in, 35–37, 39, 66–67, 172; teaching of, 31–43, 90, 120, 142, 144; wisdom of, 15, 31–43, 90, 142, 169, 214
BiPAP, 69–80, 182, 196
blood pressure: and brain injury, 116–20; and kidney disease, 102–6; medications for, 81–88, 183, 195, 197; overview of, 56–68, 84–88
brain death, 113–122, 207n1
brain injury: aggressive treatments for, 116, 118–19, 122, 186; caused by CPR, 56, 115, 117–19, 122, 181; overview of, 113–18, 122; treatments for, 53–56, 72, 85, 92, 94, 97–98, 118, 122
breathing machines. *See* ventilation, mechanical

Canadian Geriatrics Society, 97
cancer, 34, 56, 64, 107, 130–31, 155
cardiac arrest: cause of brain injury, 56, 115, 117–19, 122, 181; and CPR, 47–58, 181, 194; and defibrillation, 55, 81, 187, 194; overview of, 52–58, 193, 196

medical ethics, 17, 31–32, 90, 95, 119, 140–44, 157, 214
mercy killing, 23, 62, 128, 132, 147, 166. *See also* euthanasia
miracles, 36–37
morphine, 135
mortality: Christian view of, 36, 57, 136, 159–60, 213; in dialysis patients, 105–7, 111; in hospitalized patients, 50, 53–56, 104–7, 130–33, 145–46, 182; in ICU patients, 61, 64, 76, 203n2; in ventilated patients, 75–76, 182
murder, 23, 62, 128, 132, 147, 166. *See also* euthanasia
myocardial infarction, 52, 195. *See also* heart attack

narcotics, 72, 132, 135
nasogastric (NG) tubes, 93–94, 96, 195
National Hospice and Palliative Care Organization (NHPCO), 155, 209n7, 214
Nightingale, Florence, 61
noninvasive positive pressure ventilation (NIPPV), 77–78, 182, 196

organ failure, 16, 83–84, 87, 101
organ-supporting measures: discontinuation of, 60, 132, 139–47, 163, 193; effect on cure, 17, 34–35, 41, 62, 67, 125, 129
oxygen, 51–58, 71–73, 84, 113, 115–18, 183, 194–97

pain: of aggressive treatments, 22–25, 32, 35, 38, 64, 75, 96, 132–37, 181; of death, 15, 32, 35, 135, 142–47, 155–64, 171; medications for, 85, 132, 135, 137; of terminal illness, 22, 41–42, 97, 106, 135, 142–47, 155–64, 187; of unconscious patients, 97, 118, 122
palliative care, 27, 96, 125–37, 142, 146, 155, 194–96, 214

panic, 15, 41, 63, 71, 74, 76, 96, 134
Parkinson's disease, 94
Paul (the apostle), 18, 32–33, 39–40, 65, 121, 144, 152
percutaneous endoscopic gastrostomy (PEG), 94
permanent unconsciousness, 113–24, 121, 155, 187
persistent vegetative state, 56, 97, 113–24, 163, 187
pharynx, 71, 196
physician orders for life-sustaining treatment (POLST), 154–55, 185, 196, 211n7, 214
physician-assisted suicide (PAS), 34, 38, 132, 135, 139–47, 196. *See also* euthanasia
platelets, 103, 196
pleural effusion, 73, 196
pneumonia, 56, 62, 64, 73–77, 93, 95, 109, 118, 182, 196
pneumothorax, 196
polio, 61
POLST. *See* physician orders for life-sustaining treatment
post-traumatic stress disorder (PTSD), 41, 64, 67, 129–30, 196
prayer: guidance at end of life, 18, 42, 56, 110, 121, 129, 139, 152, 162, 168, 176; for healing, 36–37, 121; hindrances to, 25, 65, 125, 134, 152, 158, 177; of Jesus Christ, 36–37, 172
psychiatric illness, 64, 129, 196
pulmonary edema, 73, 196

Satan, 67, 142
Schiavo, Terri, 89, 97, 205n1 (chap. 7)
sedation: for brain injury, 116; for cardioversion, 55; for dialysis, 107; in the ICU, 63, 143; for mechanical ventilation, 26–27, 74–80, 92, 182; for pain, 72, 85, 135; with voluntary active euthanasia (VAE), 139
self-determination, 32, 141, 144, 157, 193. *See also* autonomy

SCRIPTURE INDEX